Poetry Speaks! Student Workbook

A Guide for Reading, Interpreting, and Enjoying Poetry

Grades 9-12

Jamie Collins

Shake Shock Press
Phoenix, AZ

All contents Copyright © 2021 by Jamie Collins for Shake Shock Press. All rights reserved. No part of this book may be reproduced, translated, stored in a retrieval system, or transmitted in any form or by any means, (electronic, mechanical, photocopying, recording, or otherwise) without prior written permission of the author.

Limit of Liability and Disclaimer of Warranty: The publisher has used its best efforts in preparing this workbook, and the information provided herein is provided "as is." Jamie Collins and Shake Shock Press make no representation or warranties with respect to the accuracy or completeness of the contents of this workbook and specifically disclaims any implied warranties of merchantability or fitness for any particular purpose and shall in no event be liable for any loss of profit or any other commercial damage, including but not limited to special, incidental, consequential, or other damages.

Photocopying of student worksheets by a classroom teacher at a non-profit school who has purchased this publication for his/her own class is permissible. Reproduction of any part of this publication for an entire school or for a school system, by for-profit institutions and tutoring centers, or for commercial sale is strictly prohibited.

Cover Design by: Kim Killion

Interior Design by: Damonza

"No verse is free for the man who wants to do a good job."

~ T.S. Eliot

Table of Contents

What Do You Know? 1
    Anticipation Activity 3
    How to Read a Poem 4
    The First Read 5
    The Second Read 8
    Three Main Poetic Forms 10

The Shakespearean Sonnet 11
    The First Read 12
    The Second Read 14
    After Reading Questions 16
    After Reading Questions 17
    Writing Exercise 18

Hip Hop 19
    The First Read 21
    The Second Read 23
    After Reading Questions 25
    After Reading Questions 26
    Hip Hop vs. Traditional Poetry 28
    Write Your Own Rap Song 29
    Write Your Own Rap Song 30

Ode and Elegy 31
    The First Read 33
    The Second Read 35
    Writing Exercise 37
    Writing Exercise 38
    Social Media Post – Grecian Urn for Sale! 39
    Social Media Post – Grecian Urn for Sale! 40

Elegy 41
    The First Read 42
    The Second Read 44
    Poem Translation 46
    Comprehension Questions 48
    Writing Exercise 50
    An Elegy for...? 52

Narrative Poem 54
    The First Read 56
    The Second Read 58
    After Reading Questions 61
    After Reading Questions 62

    Podcast Interview: Edgar Allen Poe 63
Dramatic Monologue 64
    The First Read 67
    The Second Read 69
    Line Analysis 71
    Critical Thinking Questions 73
    Poem Summary 74
    Critical Thinking Questions 76
    Pick a Persona – Journal Writing 78
Concrete Poems 81
    Your Turn! 84
Haiku 86
    Your Turn! 88
Free Verse 90
    The First Read 92
    The Second Read 94
    Short Answer Questions 96
    After Reading Questions 97
    Write Your Own Free Verse Poem 98
    Write Your Free Verse Poem 99
    Poetry Exam (Grades 9-10) 100
    Poetry Exam (Grades 11-12) 108
    Additional Templates & Forms: Journal Writing 124
Journal Writing 125
Literary Terms Study Guide 127
Answer Key 131
Rubric for Literary Paragraph 145
Resource: Literary Terms 146

A Note to Parents/Guardians/Instructors

My name is Jamie Collins and I have developed this workbook with a love of literature in mind. As a teacher and author, it is no secret that I revere the art of communication—of story telling, and of words, in all forms and fashion.

Poetry, in particular is a gift that the reader has the pleasure of unwrapping again and again, each time unveiling new and limitless discovery. The ***Poetry Speaks! Student Workbook*** offers a general study of both contemporary and traditional poetry styles. It explores conventions and analysis of poetic devices, and offers fun and useful methods for how to effectively read and evaluate poems.

Now, more than ever it is a great time to learn and to explore the timeless tenants of language arts— in or out of the classroom—in a 21st century world.

The benefits of this workbook will help your student to:

- Develop close reading skills necessary to promote comprehension and appreciation for poetry.
- Identify key literary elements in poems such as: similes, metaphors, imagery, alliteration, end-stopped lines, form, rhythm, and symbolism.
- Recognize and explain different types of poetry and their purpose.
- Compare and contrast poetic styles in terms of conveying certain moods, motifs, and themes.
- Experience various forms of poetry for introspection and enjoyment.

I do hope that your student will embrace this learning journey and that you, too will find it easy and rewarding to champion. Having a supportive hand along the way can make all the difference. Feel free to dive in with them in the discovery and the wonder!

Warmest regards,

~ Jamie Collins

Dear Student,

Where do you experience poetry? Actually, it can be anywhere from song lyrics on your smartphone to greeting cards, bumper stickers, or brand slogans that you cannot get out of your head. It's the thing that makes you tap your foot to a drop beat in a song, or punch your fist to a refrain that rings like an anthem in your soul. It's when words move you and make you *feel* something.

This can be any emotion, really, so be prepared to be moved when you read a poem in this workbook; either to happiness, sorrow, anger, patriotism, regret, or wonder. It doesn't matter what evokes that "emotional response," it only matters that it *does*.

Our aim here is to keep it simple and straightforward. For instance, how can you take what you already know about **literary devices** and apply that to the poems here before you? This workbook contains a **Resource List** to make it a bit easier to review those devices, and see them in action, so that you can become proficient at finding them in the wild.

But identifying the structure and mechanics is only one aspect of analyzing a poem. It goes much deeper than that and that is why we give each poem a thorough **close read**, several times, so that you can find those hidden gems in the meaning – the poet's gift, so to speak. That way, you can make connections that can become the "magic dust" that writing a stellar literary analysis is all about. It will help you to draft critiques that will more than make the grade.

There are many types of poems; too many to cover here. We will, however, take a look at several different types in this workbook for mix and variety. We will dive into some techniques that will help you to read, interpret, and appreciate the literary form, today, and for years to come. Becoming well versed in poetry is more than just memorizing rules; it's about noticing the poet's intentions and experiencing how a work makes you *feel*.

Don't worry, I will walk you through it all, and who knows? It might even inspire you to find a new mode of expression for yourself. So, let's get to it!

~ JC

Name: _____   Poetry Speaks!
                                   Activity #1: Quick Starter Quiz

What Do You Know?

Take a few minutes to answer each question based on the knowledge *you currently have*.

1. How many types of poems can you list? (The first one is done for you).

   a. *free verse*

   b.

   c.

   d.

2. Name a famous poet, living or deceased. _____

3. True or False. Hip Hop is a type of poetry. Circle the correct answer: **T / F.**

4. Name any three **literary devices** associated with poetry.

   a.

   b.

   c.

5. A **Haiku** is a type of poem that is comprised of how many lines?

   a. one

   b. twelve

   c. three

   d. two

6. Fill in the blank.

   In general, poetry can be divided into three main poetic **forms**. These are Lyric, Narrative, and _____.

Name: _____

Poetry Speaks!
Activity #1: Quick Starter Quiz

7. When reading a poem for the first time, what are some things you might have "questions" about?

   Example: *What does the title convey?*

   a.

   b.

   c.

8. Do you have to agree with the ideas expressed in a poem? Check one:

   _____ Yes, always
   _____ No
   _____ Not sure

BONUS QUESTIONS: What stumps you the most when reading/analyzing poetry? What would you most like to learn about the study and appreciation of poetry? Jot your thoughts down here or in your own poetry/writing journal:

Name: _____

Poetry Speaks!
Activity #2: Free Write

Anticipation Activity

Definition: Free writing: *A type of prewriting exercise or automatic writing in which a person writes freely without concern for accuracy of conventions (grammar, spelling, punctuation, etc.) in an effort to get ideas onto the page.*

Directions:

Free write your thoughts about poetry here. How does it make you feel? Does it matter? Why or why not?

_____

_____

_____

_____

_____

_____

_____

_____

_____

_____

© Shake Shock Press   Copyright material

Name: _____

Poetry Speaks!
How to Read a Poem – All Grade Levels

How to Read a Poem

There is no magic formula for approaching a poem that will grant you the keys to total understanding. In fact, it will take multiple readings to unlock the many concepts and nuances of any poem. Poetry is an art form, and by virtue of that fact, analysis is open to *interpretation*.

That said, it is also important to approach the task armed with your knowledge of conventions of English and a comprehension of **literary terms** (see resource at the back of this workbook), in addition to your distinctive thoughts and emotions.

In this workbook, we will take a **3 Step Approach** to delving into a poem that basically breaks down to this:

- ✓ **The First Read**
- ✓ **The Second Read**
- ✓ **The "Gut Check"**

Of course, there will be questions, writing activities, quizzes, and lesson extensions, but once you become comfortable knowing *what* to look for and ***how*** to frame your impressions and understanding, you will have this whole poetry thing in the bag.

So, let's dive in!

Name: _____

Poetry Speaks!
Activity #3: All grade levels

The First Read

Read the poem straight though. Feel free to read it out loud. Take notice of the title, its shape on the page, the number of stanzas (if any), and/or any other notable surface features. Is it long? Short? Are there any notable patterns? Unfamiliar words? What type of poem is it?

Locker Riot

By Jamie Collins

Behind this combination there should be shame.
But instead it is my own creation.
Books sideways and teetering on a laptop case,
Binders bulging with—formulas and free verse.
Packets of Skittles, one sock, and a purse.
I am quite proud of the craft and the care,
Of the tiny beaded chandelier that I placed there.
Among the stickers and glitter and glam
My secret space screams who I am.
One plastic Dollar Store mirror on the door,
Lip color check, hair clip tight—confidence borderline.
A magnet stuck high above,
A hundred times reminds me of
The person I am; a riddle to be solved by none.
Because I got this, and I can do no wrong!

SOURCE: SHACK SHOCK PRESS

Name: _____   "Locker Riot"
                                                Activity #3: All grade levels

There is so much to look for at first glance. You might wish to make some quick notes as you read through the text the first time. You can mark up the poem with notes, line numbers, highlights, and/or rhyme scheme labels.

Consider using a chart like the sample below in which to record your <u>initial thoughts and impressions</u> either while reading or after.

Model Chart entries for the poem, "Locker Riot":

Passage(s):	Line(s) or Stanza:	Observations, Questions, Literary Device(s)
"Locker Riot"	Title	*This is curious; what type of locker is this?*
"Behind this combination there should be shame." "Books sideways and teetering on a laptop case."	Line 1 Line 3	*The tone is very casual and the speaker appears to be a teen. Is this a school locker?*

Your Turn!

Use the blank chart on the following page to add your own entries as you read through the poem for the first time. Feel free to make copies of it if you need more space to capture your notes. Some things you might want to take note of:

- ✓ What does the title suggest?
- ✓ How does the language impact the mood or tone?
- ✓ How do the lines or stanzas stack up? Is there a pattern?
- ✓ Is the poem enjoyable? How does it make you feel? Why?

What is your "Likability" Score of this poem (on a scale of 1 to 10 with ten being the highest? _____.

© Shake Shock Press   Copyright material

Name: _____ "Locker Riot"
Activity #3 -- First Read Note Chart

First Read Note Chart

Passage(s):	Line(s) or Stanza:	Observations, Questions, Literary Device(s)

Name: _____

"Locker Riot"
Activity #4: All grade levels

The Second Read

Now it's time to read the poem once again, this time, paying special attention to the use of imagery and/or any literary devices used (see **resource list** in the back of this workbook). Once again, you may choose instead to make your notations directly onto the poem. Or, you can use a chart like the one below to help you keep track of your impressions and/or questions.

Model Chart entries for the poem, "Locker Riot":

Passage(s):	Line(s) or Stanza:	Observations, Questions, Literary Device(s)
"**B**ehind this combination there should be shame. / **B**ut instead it is my own creation. **B**ooks sideways and teetering on a laptop case, / **B**inders **b**ulging with—formulas and free verse."	Lines 1-4	Here is **alliteration** as the "B" sound is repeated in close order. Accelerates the pacing.
"I am quite proud of the craft and the care, / Of the tiny beaded chandelier that I placed there."	Lines 6-7	Some internal rhyme but not consistent. Is this free verse?
"The person I am; a riddle to be solved by none.	Line 14	The speaker is indicating individuality and suggests that there is peace in the chaos to be found.

Your Turn!

- ✓ Summarize key points.
- ✓ Note repeated words or phrases.
- ✓ Connect ideas
- ✓ What images can you visualize?

© Shake Shock Press   Copyright material

Name: _____

"Locker Riot"
Activity #4 -- Second Read Note Chart

Second Read Note Chart

Passage(s):	Line(s) or Stanza:	Observations, Questions, Literary Device(s)

© Shake Shock Press — Copyright material

Name: _____

Poetry Speaks!
Mini Lesson #1: Three Poetic Forms

Three Main Poetic Forms

There are literally over 150 different *types* of poems identified that range from traditional, to contemporary types, to very current forms that are fun and new (nonce) that spring up from a particular purpose or occasion.

Here, we are going to group some of the poems we will be working with into three distinct categories that you will see coming up: **Lyric, Narrative, and Dramatic.** Here is a breakdown:

Main Type:	Definition:	Example(s):
Lyric	A type of poetry, often with songlike qualities that addresses the speaker's feelings and emotions. Originally intended to be sung. These include the sonnet, the ode, and the elegy.	Shakespeare's, "Sonnet 130" John Keats', "Ode on a Grecian Urn" Walt Whitman's, "O Captain! My Captain!" (Elegy for President Lincoln)
Narrative	A form of poetry that tells a story through verse. It has a plot, characters, and a setting much like a novel. Usually written in metered verse.	Homer's, *The Odyssey* (Epic Narrative) Edgar Allen Poe's, "Annabel Lee" (Ballad)
Dramatic	A type of poetry written specifically to be performed. It conveys a story, which can be either recited or sung. It is lyrical in nature. The speaker addresses an imaginary listener.	Robert Browning's, "My Last Duchess" (Dramatic Monologue)

Name: _____

Poetry Speaks!
The Sonnet - All Grade Levels

The Shakespearean Sonnet

Introduction: A sonnet is a precisely organized poem with a specific rhythmic pattern of stressed and unstressed syllables in each of its lines. A Shakespearean sonnet is a fourteen-line poem written in iambic pentameter. Three quatrains, four lines each, and a couplet (2 lines) usually forming a conclusion.

Type: Lyric

Literary Focus: Rhyme scheme: ABAB, CDCD, EFEF, GG

Vocabulary:

damasked (vb) – to decorate as with a rich pattern.

belied (vb) – to betray, disguise, or contradict.

Sonnet 130: My Mistress' Eyes Are Nothing Like the Sun
By William Shakespeare

My mistress' eyes are nothing like the sun;
Coral is far more red than her lips' red;
If snow be white, why then her breasts are dun;
If hairs be wires, black wires grow on her head.
I have seen roses damasked, red and white,
But no such roses see I in her cheeks;
And in some perfumes is there more delight
Than in the breath that from my mistress reeks.
I love to hear her speak, yet well I know
That music hath a far more pleasing sound;
I grant I never saw a goddess go;
My mistress, when she walks, treads on the ground.
And yet, by heaven, I think my love as rare
As any she belied with false compare.

SOURCE: POETRY FOUNDATION.ORG

Name: _____

Poetry Speaks!
Activity #5 – "Sonnet 130"- First Read
All Grade Levels

The First Read

Read the poem straight though. Feel free to read it out loud. Take notice of the rhyme scheme (ABAB, CDCD, EFEF, GG). Can you identify it? You might want to mark the pattern by placing the letters at the end of each line. Note how the poem is structured.

Model Chart entries for the poem, "Sonnet 130":

Passage(s):	Line(s) or Stanza:	Observations, Questions, Literary Device(s)
"And in some perfumes there is more delight"	Line 7	*What does he mean by this?*
"And yet, by heaven, I think my love as rare / As any she belied with false compare."	Lines 13-14	*This is a couplet. Both <u>rare</u> and <u>compare</u> rhyme.*

Your Turn!

Use the blank chart on the following page to add your own entries as you read through the poem for the first time. Feel free to make copies of it if you need more space to capture your notes. Some things you might want to take note of:

- ✓ Why was this written? For whom?
- ✓ How does the language impact the mood or tone?
- ✓ Can you find examples of imagery?
- ✓ What is the overall message the poet is trying to convey?

What is your "Likability" Score of this poem (on a scale of 1 to 10 with ten being the highest? _____.

© Shake Shock Press   Copyright material

Name: _____   "Sonnet 130"
Activity #5 -- First Read Note Chart

First Read Note Chart

Passage(s):	Line(s) or Stanza:	Observations, Questions, Literary Device(s)

Name: _____

Poetry Speaks!
Activity #6 - The Sonnet – Second Read
All grade levels

The Second Read

Now it's time to read the poem once again, this time, paying special attention to the use of imagery and/or any literary devices used (see **resource list** in the back of this workbook). Once again, you may choose instead to make your notations directly onto the poem. Or, you can use a chart like the one below to help you keep track of your impressions and/or questions.

Model Chart entries for the poem, "Sonnet 130":

Passage(s):	Line(s) or Stanza:	Observations, Questions, Literary Device(s)
"My mistress' eyes are nothing **like** the sun;/Coral is far more red **than** her lips' red."	Lines 1- 2	*Here the poet is using simile to convey the comparison.*
"If hairs be wires, black wires grow on her head."	Line 4	*Hyperbole*

Your Turn!

- ✓ Summarize key points.
- ✓ Note repeated words or phrases.
- ✓ Connect ideas
- ✓ What images can you visualize?

Name: _____ "Sonnet 130"
Activity #6 -- Second Read Note Chart

Second Read Note Chart

Passage(s):	Line(s) or Stanza:	Observations, Questions, Literary Device(s)

Name: _____

"Sonnet 130"
Activity #7: After Reading Questions
Grades 9-10

After Reading Questions

Refer to your charts and to the text directly when you answer the following questions below. You may need to read the poem through several more times to locate key items.

Answer (T) true or (F) false for the following statements:

1. _____ The main theme of the poem is that the speaker loves his mistress, as she is, flaws and all.

2. _____ "Coral is far more red than her lips' red" is an example of Alliteration.

3. _____ (Lines 5 – 8) The speaker's mistress has a pleasant flush to her cheeks.

4. _____ Throughout the sonnet, the speaker elevates his beloved above all other women.

5. _____ (Lines 9-12) The speaker says that he loves to listen to her voice, yet he admits that music is more pleasing than her speech.

Short Answer: Respond to the following questions. Be sure to use full sentences:

6. On a separate sheet of paper, write the meaning of each line in your own words. Do this all the way through the poem. Ex. (Line 1-2) - *My mistress' eyes are not beautiful like the sun; coral is far redder than her lips are red.*

Name: _____

"Sonnet 130"
Activity #7: After Reading Questions
Grades 11-12

After Reading Questions

Refer to your charts and to the text directly when you answer the following questions below. You may need to read the poem through several more times to locate key items.

Write your reply to each question below in 3-5 full sentences. Be sure to use proper grammar and punctuation:

1. The speaker is comparing his beloved to aspects of nature, but not in a way that exalts her. Can you find an example of this?

   _____

   _____

2. If other poets of Shakespeare's time frequently compared their beloved to the beauty of nature and goddesses, what might be the reason that he chooses to focus on her flaws?

   _____

   _____

3. What broader theme can be taken from this sonnet in regard to love and beauty?

   _____

   _____

4. What is the speaker saying in the final 2 lines (couplet) about the "comparisons" that he has made?

   _____

   _____

© Shake Shock Press — Copyright material

Name: _____

"Sonnet 130"
Activity #8: Create a Sonnet
All Grades

Writing Exercise

Now it is your turn to try your hand at creating a Shakespearean sonnet! Below are some words and phrases to help get you going. Choose **one** to focus on as a theme for your sonnet. You can prewrite your initial ideas on a separate paper and then place your 14-line polished sonnet here below:

Love	**Time**	**Struggle**
Aging	**Failure**	**Hope**
Beauty	**Pride**	**Excess**

Sonnet: (Title)
By (Your Name)

_____
_____
_____
_____
_____
_____
_____
_____
_____
_____
_____
_____
_____
_____

Name: _____

Poetry Speaks!
Hip Hop - All Grade Levels

Hip Hop

Introduction: As already stated, there are many different forms of poetry, but did you know that Hip Hop was one of them? Hip Hop and poetry have much in common that can include attention to rhythm in lyrics, end rhyme, slant rhyme, internal rhyme, alliteration, assonance, use of repetition, manipulation of language to convey powerful emotions, and/or choice of diction. Some Hip Hop lyrics are controversial.

Biography: Nikki Giovanni (1943 -) is an American poet, writer and activist. She was a participant in the Black Arts movement of the late 1960s.

Type: Lyric

Style: Rap artists often write in sixteen-bar stanzas, normally followed by four-to-eight bar hooks.

Vocabulary: A focus on urban slang.

Ego Tripping (there may be a reason why)
By Nikki Giovanni

I was born in the Congo
I walked to the Fertile Crescent and built
The Sphinx
I designed a pyramid so tough that a star
That only glows every one hundred years falls
Into the center giving divine perfect light
I am bad

I sat on the throne
Drinking nectar with Allah
I got hot and sent an ice age to Europe
To cool my thirst
My oldest daughter is Nefertiti
The tears from my birth pains
Created the Nile
I am a beautiful woman

© Shake Shock Press
Copyright material

Name: _____

Poetry Speaks!
Hip Hop - All Grade Levels

I gazed on the forest and burned
Out the Sahara desert
With a packet of goat's meat
And a change of clothes
I crossed it in two hours
I am a gazelle so swift
So swift you can't catch me

For a birthday present when he was three
I gave my son Hannibal an elephant
He gave me Rome for mother's day
My strength flows ever on

My son Noah built New/Ark and
I stood proudly at the helm
As we sailed on a soft summer day
I turned myself into myself and was
Jesus
Men intone my loving name
All praises All praises
I am the one who would save

I sowed diamonds in my back yard
My bowels deliver uranium
The filings from my fingernails are
Semi-precious jewels
On a trip north
I caught a cold and blew
My nose giving oil to the Arab world
I am so hip even my errors are correct
I sailed west to reach east and had to round off
The earth as I went
The hair from my head thinned and gold was laid
Across three continents

I am so perfect so divine so ethereal so surreal
I cannot be comprehended except by my permission

I mean...I can fly
Like a bird in the sky

Source: Genius.com

Name: _____

Poetry Speaks!
Activity #9 – "Ego Tripping"- First Read
All Grade Levels

The First Read

Read the poem straight though. Feel free to read it out loud. Imagine this put to a rap beat. Take notice of the rhyme scheme. Is there one? How do the words work to create a rhythm? Can you find internal rhyme? What effect does it have on the poem?

Model Chart entries for the poem, "Ego Tripping":

Passage(s):	Line(s) or Stanza:	Observations, Questions, Literary Device(s)
Who is the speaker in this poem?	Stanza 1-8	*Not sure how one being can do all of this. This is a female.*
"The tears from my birth pains Created the Nile"	Stanza 2	*This is hyperbole. Not to be taken literally.* *There does not appear to be a distinct rhyme scheme.*

Your Turn!

Use the blank chart on the following page to add your own entries as you read through the poem for the first time. Feel free to make copies of it if you need more space to capture your notes. Some things you might want to take note of:

- ✓ What is the significance of the title?
- ✓ How does the language contribute to the poem's impact?
- ✓ What do all of the images/figures have in common?
- ✓ What is the central message or theme?

What is your "Likability" Score of this poem (on a scale of 1 to 10 with ten being the highest? _____.

Name: _____

"Ego Tripping"
Activity #9 -- First Read Note Chart

First Read Note Chart

Passage(s):	Line(s) or Stanza:	Observations, Questions, Literary Device(s)

Name: _____

Poetry Speaks!
Activity #10 – "Ego Tripping" - Second Read
All grade levels

The Second Read

Now it's time to read the poem once again, this time, paying special attention to the use of imagery and/or any literary devices used (see **resource list** in the back of this workbook). Once again, you may choose instead to make your notations directly onto the poem. Or, you can use a chart like the one below to help you keep track of your impressions and/or questions.

Model Chart entries for the poem, "Ego Tripping":

Passage(s):	Line(s) or Stanza:	Observations, Questions, Literary Device(s)
"As we sailed on a soft summer day"	Stanza 5	*The alliterative use of the soft syllable "s" in this line mimics the smooth sensation of sailing on calm waters.*
"I stood proudly at the helm"	Stanza 5	*The previous line, by contrast features "hard" consonant sounds affecting the change in rhythm.*

Your Turn!

- ✓ Summarize key points.
- ✓ Note repeated words or phrases.
- ✓ Connect ideas
- ✓ What images can you visualize?

© Shake Shock Press · Copyright material

Name: _____ "Ego Tripping"
Activity #10 -- Second Read Note Chart

Second Read Note Chart

Passage(s):	Line(s) or Stanza:	Observations, Questions, Literary Device(s)

Name: _____

"Ego Tripping"
Activity #11: After Reading Questions
Grades 9-10

After Reading Questions

Refer to your charts and to the text directly when you answer the following questions below. You may need to read the poem through several more times to locate key items.

Short Answer: Respond to the following questions. Be sure to use full sentences:

1. What does the title, "Ego Tripping" imply?

2. Who is the speaker, or the "I" in the poem? How do you know?

3. List some of the supernatural elements in the poem.

4. Repetition is a characteristic of Hip Hop / poetry. Repeating the word, "so" in the line, "I am *so* perfect *so* divine *so* ethereal *so* surreal" works to do what in the poem?

5. Do you think that this poem reflects any current themes that might take on new meaning in today's world?

© Shake Shock Press   Copyright material

Name: _____

"Ego Tripping"
Activity #11: After Reading Questions
Grades 11-12

After Reading Questions

Refer to your charts and to the text directly when you answer the following questions below. You may need to read the poem through several more times to locate key items.

Write your reply to each question below in 5-10 sentences. Remember to use proper grammar and punctuation:

1. The speaker of the poem takes on the role of creator, or a divinely powerful being. Find some examples from the poem that show this and explain how they support her proclamation.

2. The poem has no rhyme scheme or meter pattern, but it is the *rhythm* of the poem that is distinct. The irregularity of the lines contributes to giving the words a musical quality. Can you find some examples?

3. References to Egyptian imagery was a common trait in poems by Harlem Renaissance as well as contemporary writers. Find and list as many Egyptian references as you can in this poem.

© Shake Shock Press

Name: _____

"Ego Tripping"
Activity #11: After Reading Questions
Grades 11-12

4. Poets like Langston Hughes and Nikki Giovanni referenced history to embrace their African heritage. How does this aspect add to the tone of the poem, "Ego Tripping?"

5. How do phrases such as, "I am bad" and "I am hip" contribute to the poem?

6. What would you say is the prevailing theme of this poem? Why?

7. Do you think that this poem reflects any current themes that might take on new meaning in today's world? Explain.

Name: _____

Poetry Speaks!
Mini Lesson #2: Hip Hop vs. Traditional Poetry
All Grade Levels

Hip Hop vs. Traditional Poetry

People have been relaying stories in a poetic or musical way for as far back as the time of Homer (the late eighth or early seventh century BC). As stated, there are many forms of "poetry" ranging from the traditional to the new and contemporary forms. Let's take a look at how **Hip Hop** and **Traditional Poetry** compare to one another:

Characteristic	Hip Hop:	Traditional Poetry:
Use of Rhythm or a beat to convey a message. Some phrases make no sense.	Yes	Yes
Use of Rhyme, Symbolism, Alliteration, Consonance as a technique.	Often (but not mandatory)	Often (but not mandatory)
How conveyed to the listener?	Most often performed.	Written down and read or recited.
Relies on music (rapping) to accentuate the rhythm.	Yes	No (relies on the person reading to identify the rhythm)
Uses language to convey something beyond the literal meaning of the words.	Yes (Often themes about crime, violence, or oppression)	Yes (Often themes about love, beauty, or truth)

© Shake Shock Press   Copyright material

Name: _____

"Ego Tripping"
Activity #12: Pre-Writing Exercise
All Grades

Write Your Own Rap Song

Have you ever dreamt of being the next Dr. Dre or Snoop Dogg? Music is powerful. Its lyrics and themes can help connect people to ideas, a cause, or one another. Now is your chance to put those song-writing skills to work by coming up with your very own masterpiece!

What makes a great rap song? Use of literary devices, a notable beat or rhythm, a humorous/memorable "punch" line, and a powerful underlying message.

Prompt: Write your own creative work on the theme of overcoming challenges in the Hip Hop style.

Use this space for your brainstorming and prewriting ideas first:

Name: _____

"Ego Tripping"
Activity #13: Writing Exercise
All Grades

Write Your Own Rap Song

[Title]
By [Your Name]

Name: _____

Poetry Speaks!
Mini Lesson #3 – Ode and Elegy
All Grades

Ode and Elegy

Two additional lyrical forms of poetry are the **Ode** and the **Elegy**.

Ode: A serious or thoughtful poem that is written to pay homage to someone or something. It is written in a formal structure; often elevated in style. It includes some sub-genres of sonnets. Can be set to music, but not always. **Example:** John Keats,' "Ode On a Grecian Urn".

Ode On a Grecian Urn
By John Keats (1795-1821)

Thou still unravish'd bride of quietness,
    Thou foster-child of silence and slow time,
Sylvan historian, who canst thus express
    A flowery tale more sweetly than our rhyme:
What leaf-fring'd legend haunts about thy shape
    Of deities or mortals, or of both,
        In Tempe or the dales of Arcady?
    What men or gods are these? What maidens loth?
What mad pursuit? What struggle to escape?
        What pipes and timbrels? What wild ecstasy?

Heard melodies are sweet, but those unheard
    Are sweeter; therefore, ye soft pipes, play on;
Not to the sensual ear, but, more endear'd,
    Pipe to the spirit ditties of no tone:
Fair youth, beneath the trees, thou canst not leave
    Thy song, nor ever can those trees be bare;
        Bold Lover, never, never canst thou kiss,
Though winning near the goal yet, do not grieve;
    She cannot fade, though thou hast not thy bliss,
        For ever wilt thou love, and she be fair!

Name: _____

Poetry Speaks!
Mini Lesson #3 – Ode and Elegy
• All Grades

Ah, happy, happy boughs! that cannot shed
    Your leaves, nor ever bid the Spring adieu;
And, happy melodist, unwearied,
    For ever piping songs for ever new;
More happy love! more happy, happy love!
    For ever warm and still to be enjoy'd,
        For ever panting, and for ever young;
All breathing human passion far above,
    That leaves a heart high-sorrowful and cloy'd,
        A burning forehead, and a parching tongue.

Who are these coming to the sacrifice?
    To what green altar, O mysterious priest,
Lead'st thou that heifer lowing at the skies,
    And all her silken flanks with garlands drest?
What little town by river or sea shore,
    Or mountain-built with peaceful citadel,
        Is emptied of this folk, this pious morn?
And, little town, thy streets for evermore
    Will silent be; and not a soul to tell
        Why thou art desolate, can e'er return.

O Attic shape! Fair attitude! with brede
    Of marble men and maidens overwrought,
With forest branches and the trodden weed;
    Thou, silent form, dost tease us out of thought
As doth eternity: Cold Pastoral!
    When old age shall this generation waste,
        Thou shalt remain, in midst of other woe
Than ours, a friend to man, to whom thou say'st,
    "Beauty is truth, truth beauty,—that is all
        Ye know on earth, and all ye need to know."

Source: poetryfoundation.org

Name: _____

Poetry Speaks!
Activity #14 – "Ode On a Grecian Urn"- First Read
All Grade Levels

The First Read

Keats is addressing the theme of the immortality of art and beauty in this poem. The speaker is fixated; it seems, on the images carved into the urn of unnamed people who are locked in time. He ponders the differences between their world and that of the observer in the real world.

Model Chart entries for the poem, "Ode On a Grecian Urn":

Passage(s):	Line(s) or Stanza:	Observations, Questions, Literary Device(s)
"Thou still unravish'd bride of quietness, / Thou foster-child of silence and slow time"	Stanza 1	Who is the speaker addressing?
"Fair youth," "Bold Lover," and later, "These coming to sacrifice"	Stanzas 2 & 4	Who are the people mentioned on the urn?

Your Turn!

Use the blank chart on the following page to add your own entries as you read through the poem for the first time. Feel free to make copies of it if you need more space to capture your notes. Some things you might want to take note of:

- ✓ Does this poem have a structure or pattern? What is it?
- ✓ Who is the speaker?
- ✓ How are the different people depicted on the urn?
- ✓ What conclusions does the speaker make?
- ✓ What is the central message or theme?

What is your "Likability" Score of this poem (on a scale of 1 to 10 with ten being the highest? ____.

Name: _____

"Ode On a Grecian Urn"
Activity #14 - First Read Note Chart

First Read Note Chart

Passage(s):	Line(s) or Stanza:	Observations, Questions, Literary Device(s)

Name: _____   Poetry Speaks!
Activity #15 – "Ode On a Grecian Urn"– Second Read
All grade levels

The Second Read

Now it's time to read the poem once again, this time, paying special attention to the use of imagery and/or any literary devices used (see **resource list** in the back of this workbook). Once again, you may choose instead to make your notations directly onto the poem. Or, you can use a chart like the one below to help you keep track of your impressions and/or questions.

Model Chart entries for the poem, "Ode On a Grecian Urn":

Passage(s):	Line(s) or Stanza:	Observations, Questions, Literary Device(s)
"O mysterious priest" and "O Attic shape!"	Stanzas 4-5	This is an example of **apostrophe** as the speaker is addressing an inanimate object.
"**l**eaf-fring'd **l**egend," ye soft **p**ipes, **p**lay on," "**h**eart **h**igh-sorrowful"	Stanzas 1-3	**Alliteration**.

Your Turn!

- ✓ Summarize key points.
- ✓ Note repeated words or phrases.
- ✓ Connect ideas
- ✓ What images can you visualize?

© Shake Shock Press   Copyright material

Name: _____

"Ode On a Grecian Urn"
Activity #15 -- Second Read Note Chart

Second Read Note Chart

Passage(s):	Line(s) or Stanza:	Observations, Questions, Literary Device(s)

© Shake Shock Press — Copyright material

Name: _____

"Ode On a Grecian Urn"
Activity #16: Literary Analysis Paragraph
Grades 9-10

Writing Exercise

Using your notes, write a one paragraph literary analysis based on the prompt given. You can prewrite your initial ideas on a separate paper and then place your 8-10 sentence, polished final paragraph here below. (See general writing rubric at the back).

Prompt: The title, "Ode On a Grecian Urn," gives the reader an idea about what the poem is about. What is the central idea and how does the poet use imagery to convey it?

- Write 8-10 well-formed sentences.
- Correct use of conventions, sentence structure, and syntax; spelling & grammar.
- Formal / Objective tone; no contractions.

Your Paragraph:

_____

_____

_____

_____

_____

_____

_____

_____

© Shake Shock Press   Copyright material

Name: _____

"Ode On a Grecian Urn"
Activity #17: Literary Analysis Paragraph
Grades 11-12

Writing Exercise

Using your notes, write a one paragraph literary analysis based on the prompt given that includes two passages from the poem, correctly cited. You can prewrite your initial ideas on a separate paper and then place your polished final paragraph here below. (See general writing Rubric at the back).

Prompt: The last two lines of the poem attempt to sum up everything in one famous couplet: *"Beauty is truth, truth is beauty"*. What does this mean in light of the speaker's attempt to contemplate the theme of the immortality of art?

- Write a correctly structured paragraph with a topic sentence, two correctly cited passages from the poem, each with commentary, and an effective concluding sentence.
- Correct use of conventions, sentence structure, and syntax; spelling & grammar.
- Formal / Objective tone; no contractions.
- Example of in-text citation: **(Keats stanza 2)**.

Your Paragraph: (Use a separate piece of paper if you need more space).

_____

_____

_____

_____

_____

_____

_____

Name: _____

Poetry Speaks!
Activity #18 – Social Media Post

Social Media Post – Grecian Urn for Sale!

Step: #1 -- Imagine that the Grecian Urn is for sale. Draw a sketch of it in keeping with the images described in Keats' poem. Use your imagination and a little research to draw the Urn as it would appear in an advertisement.

Place your drawing in the frame below:

© Shake Shock Press   Copyright material

Name: _____

Poetry Speaks!
Activity #18 – Social Media Post

Social Media Post – Grecian Urn for Sale!

Step: #2 – Next, write some ad copy to sell the Urn by creating a social media post that might cause someone to click on the item to buy it. Describe the dimensions, weight, finish, and images in as much detail as possible. Be sure to include a catchy headline! Lastly, what price would you ask for this timeless work of art?

_____

_____

_____

_____

_____

_____

_____

_____

_____

_____

_____

_____

_____

_____

_____

© Shake Shock Press   Copyright material

Name: _____

Poetry Speaks!
Activity #19: -- Ode and Elegy
All Grades

Elegy

Elegy: A sad and thoughtful poem about the death of an individual. No real rules of structure. Can be written for an actual person, or about the general subject of loss. **Example:** Walt Whitman's, "O Captain! My Captain!" (about the assassination of Abraham Lincoln).

O Captain! My Captain!
By Walt Whitman (1859-1928)

O CAPTAIN! my Captain! our fearful trip is done;
The ship has weather'd every rack, the prize we sought is won;
The port is near, the bells I hear, the people all exulting,
While follow eyes the steady keel, the vessel grim and daring:
But O heart! heart! heart!
O the bleeding drops of red,
Where on the deck my Captain lies,
Fallen cold and dead.

O Captain! my Captain! rise up and hear the bells;
Rise up--for you the flag is flung--for you the bugle trills;
For you bouquets and ribbon'd wreaths--for you the shores a-crowding;
For you they call, the swaying mass, their eager faces turning;
Here Captain! dear father!
This arm beneath your head;
It is some dream that on the deck,
You've fallen cold and dead.

My Captain does not answer, his lips are pale and still;
My father does not feel my arm, he has no pulse nor will;
The ship is anchor'd safe and sound, its voyage closed and done;
From fearful trip, the victor ship, comes in with object won;
Exult, O shores, and ring, O bells!
But I, with mournful tread,
Walk the deck my Captain lies,
Fallen cold and dead.

SOURCE: POETRYFOUNDATION.ORG

© Shake Shock Press — Copyright material

Name: _____

Poetry Speaks!
Activity #19 – "O Captain! My Captain!"
First Read -- All Grade Levels

The First Read

Walt Whitman, a patriot and supporter of unionists, wrote this tribute to the deceased Abraham Lincoln in 1865, when the Civil War was coming to an end. Whitman was greatly distraught by Lincoln's death. It is an extended metaphor poem in which the author uses the same metaphor throughout the entire work. See if you can identify this literary device in the poem.

Model Chart entries for the poem, "O Captain! My Captain!":

Passage(s):	Line(s) or Stanza:	Observations, Questions, Literary Device(s)
"But O heart! heart! heart! O the bleeding drops of red, Where on the deck my Captain lies, Fallen cold and dead"	Lines 5-8	*Repetition and rhyme*
Three stanzas – with two quatrains (4 lines) in each.	Stanzas 1-3	*A mix of free verse and some rhyming patterns. Helps to create a feeling of mourning and emotions spilling out.*

Your Turn!

Use the blank chart on the following page to add your own entries as you read through the poem for the first time. Feel free to make copies of it if you need more space to capture your notes. Some things you might want to take note of:

- ✓ How does this poem make you feel?
- ✓ Why does the poet refer to Lincoln as "Captain"?
- ✓ Are there any contrasts in the poem?
- ✓ What is the final realization expressed by the poet?

What is your "Likability" Score of this poem (on a scale of 1 to 10 with ten being the highest? ____.

© Shake Shock Press   Copyright material

Name: _____

"O Captain! My Captain!"
Activity #19 -- First Read Note Chart

First Read Note Chart

Passage(s):	Line(s) or Stanza:	Observations, Questions, Literary Device(s)

Name: _____

Poetry Speaks!
Activity #20 – "O Captain! My Captain!"
Second Read – All Grade Levels

The Second Read

Now it's time to read the poem once again, this time, paying special attention to the use of imagery and/or any literary devices used (see **resource list** in the back of this workbook). Once again, you may choose instead to make your notations directly onto the poem. Or, you can use a chart like the one below to help you keep track of your impressions and/or questions.

Model Chart entries for the poem, "O Captain! My Captain!":

Passage(s):	Line(s) or Stanza:	Observations, Questions, Literary Device(s)
"O **Captain**! my **Captain**!" and "O **Captain**! my **Captain**!" "My **Captain** does not answer…"	Stanzas 1 & 2 Stanza 3	*This is an example of **anaphora** as several verses begin with the same phrase.*
"The ship has weather'd every rack, the prize we sought is won"	Stanza 1	**Allusion** – *Here, the ship is in reference to the United States when it was on its voyage to freedom/independence.*

Your Turn!

- ✓ Summarize key points.
- ✓ Note repeated words or phrases.
- ✓ Connect ideas
- ✓ What images can you visualize?

© Shake Shock Press

Name: _____

"O Captain! My Captain!"
Activity #20 -- Second Read Note Chart

Second Read Note Chart

Passage(s):	Line(s) or Stanza:	Observations, Questions, Literary Device(s)

Name: _____

"O Captain! My Captain!"
Activity #21: Poem Translation
Grades 9-10

Poem Translation

Refer to your charts and to the text directly when you complete this assignment. Summarize the poem *in your own words*, line by line. Be sure to use proper grammar and punctuation. You should have one paragraph per stanza.

Example:

1. O Captain! my Captain! our fearful trip is done.   =   O Captain, my Captain! Our hard journey has ended. The ship has survived every storm.

2. The ship has weather'd every rack, the prize we sought is won.   =   The ship has survived every storm and we've won the prize we've been fighting for.

Name: _____

"O Captain! My Captain!"
Activity #21: Poem Translation
Grades 9-10

Name: _____

"O Captain! My Captain!"
Activity #22: Comprehension Questions
Grades 11-12

Comprehension Questions

Refer to your charts and poem's text. Answer each question by choosing **the best** response:

1. Where is the battle ship located?

    a. on the stormy waters

    b. near the port, anchored safely

    c. floating off in the distance

    d. off the shores of England

2. Who did Whitman write this poem for? _____ .

3. The people waiting for the captain have the following items EXCEPT for:

    a. bouquets

    b. bugles

    c. ribboned wreaths

    d. drums and streamers

4. Why is the speaker so distraught even though they won the battle?

    a. His captain is now dead.

    b. The cargo has been lost

    c. It is the ship's last voyage.

    d. He has been shot in the arm.

© Shake Shock Press · · · Copyright material

Name: _____

"O Captain! My Captain!"
Activity #22: Multiple Choice Questions
Grades 11-12

5. The ship in the poem is:

   a. Abraham Lincoln

   b. The United States

   c. England

   d. The Mayflower

6. What indications are there that the captain is deceased?

_____

_____

_____

_____

7. Why do you think that the speaker puts his arms beneath the captain's head?

_____

_____

_____

_____

8. What does the speaker do in the end?

   a. He joins the crowd in celebration.

   b. He covers the captain with a blanket

   c. He refuses to leave the captain.

   d. He realizes that the captain is dead and mournfully walks away.

© Shake Shock Press   Copyright material

Name: _____

"O Captain! My Captain!"
Activity #23: Literary Analysis Paragraph
All Grades

Writing Exercise

Using your notes, write a one paragraph literary analysis based on the prompt given that includes two passages from the poem, correctly cited. You can prewrite your initial ideas on a separate paper and then place your polished final paragraph here below. (See general writing Rubric at the back).

Prompt: In light of the time period in which this poem was written (just after the Civil War), discuss how the author used **the captain**, **the ship**, and **the journey** as **symbols** to convey the theme of the poem.

- Write a correctly structured paragraph with a topic sentence, two correctly cited passages from the poem, each with commentary, and an effective concluding sentence.
- Correct use of conventions, sentence structure, and syntax; spelling & grammar.
- Formal / Objective tone; no contractions.
- Example of in-text citation: **(Lines 1-2).**

Your Paragraph: (Use a separate piece of paper if you need more space).

_____

_____

_____

_____

_____

Name: _____

"O Captain! My Captain!"
Activity #23: Literary Analysis Paragraph
All Grades

Name: _____

"O Captain! My Captain!"
Activity #24: Write an Elegy – All Grades

An Elegy for...?

Time to use your writing skills for some fun! Think of a old toy, electronic gadget, TV show, food, or overused word or trend, and write an Elegy to express remorse for its passing.

Think of something gone, but not-to-be-forgotten, and try your hand at writing in a style and length of your choice. It does not have to rhyme or have a formal structure. Include as many literary devices as you can!

_____

_____

_____

_____

_____

_____

_____

_____

_____

Name: _____

"O Captain! My Captain!"
Activity #24: Write an Elegy – All Grades

Name: _____

Poetry Speaks!
Activity #25 - Narrative Poem – "Annabel Lee"
All Grade Levels

Narrative Poem

Introduction: Narrative Poetry is a form of poetry that tells a story through verse. It has a plot, characters, and a setting much like a novel. It often contains rhythmic patterns, meter, figurative language, sensory imagery, and a specific diction. One sub-category is the Ballad (a poem or song narrating a story in short stanzas).

Biography: Edgar Allen Poe is an American poet, writer, editor, and literary critic. Deemed as one of the earliest masters of the short story, Poe is best known for his tales of mystery and the macabre.

Type: Narrative / Ballad

Theme: Love and its power to enchant or destroy.

Annabel Lee
By Edgar Allen Poe (1809-1849)

It was many and many a year ago,
   In a kingdom by the sea,
That a maiden there lived whom you may know
   By the name of Annabel Lee;
And this maiden she lived with no other thought
   Than to love and be loved by me.

I was a child and *she* was a child,
   In this kingdom by the sea:
But we loved with a love that was more than love—
   I and my Annabel Lee;
With a love that the winged seraphs of heaven
   Coveted her and me.

And this was the reason that, long ago,
   In this kingdom by the sea,
A wind blew out of a cloud, chilling
   My beautiful Annabel Lee;
So that her highborn kinsman came

Name: _____   Poetry Speaks!
Activity #25 - Narrative Poem – "Annabel Lee"
All Grade Levels

    And bore her away from me,
To shut her up in a sepulchre
    In this kingdom by the sea.

The angels, not half so happy in heaven,
    Went envying her and me—
Yes!—that was the reason (as all men know,
    In this kingdom by the sea)
That the wind came out of the cloud by night,
    Chilling and killing my Annabel Lee.

But our love it was stronger by far than the love
    Of those who were older than we—
    Of many far wiser than we—
And neither the angels in heaven above,
    Nor the demons down under the sea,
Can ever dissever my soul from the soul
    Of the beautiful Annabel Lee:

For the moon never beams, without bringing me dreams
    Of the beautiful Annabel Lee;
And the stars never rise, but I feel the bright eyes
    Of the beautiful Annabel Lee;
And so, all the night-tide, I lie down by the side
Of my darling—my darling—my life and my bride,
    In her sepulchre there by the sea,
    In her tomb by the sounding sea.

SOURCE: POETS.ORG

Name: _____

Poetry Speaks!
Activity #25 – "Annabel Lee"
First Read -- All Grade Levels

The First Read

"Annabel Lee" is one of Edgar Allen Poe's last complete poems ever written, published the same year as his death. The poem is about the death of a young, beautiful woman and the speaker is her lover who is lamenting her passing. He is angry against the forces—real *and* supernatural, who tried to keep them apart. Even in death, the speaker vows that their love endures.

Model Chart entries for the poem, "Annabel Lee":

Passage(s):	Line(s) or Stanza:	Observations, Questions, Literary Device(s)
"It was many and many a year ago, / In a kingdom by the sea, / That a maiden there lived whom you may know / By the name of Annabel Lee"	Lines 1-4	*The poem opens like a fairy tale; might be a tale of fantasy.*
"In a kingdom by the sea", "Annabel Lee", and "loved by me"	Lines 2, 4, and 6	*Sets up a rhyming pattern of the long /e/ vowel sound.* *Repeated many times throughout the poem in an almost obsessive repetition.*

Your Turn!

Use the blank chart on the following page to add your own entries as you read through the poem for the first time. Feel free to make copies of it if you need more space to capture your notes. Some things you might want to take note of: How does this poem make you feel at different points?

- ✓ Can you detect a shift in mood?
- ✓ How are love, death, and grief expressed here?
- ✓ What helps to create a hypnotic effect in the poem?

What is your "Likability" Score of this poem (on a scale of 1 to 10 with ten being the highest? ____.

© Shake Shock Press   Copyright material

Name: _____

"Annabel Lee"
Activity #25 -- First Read Note Chart

First Read Note Chart

Passage(s):	Line(s) or Stanza:	Observations, Questions, Literary Device(s)

© Shake Shock Press · Copyright material

Name: _____

Poetry Speaks!
Activity #26 – "Annabel Lee"
Second Read – All Grade Levels

The Second Read

Now it's time to read the poem once again, this time, paying special attention to the use of imagery and/or any literary devices used (see **resource list** in the back of this workbook). Once again, you may choose instead to make your notations directly onto the poem. Or, you can use a chart like the one below to help you keep track of your impressions and/or questions.

Model Chart entries for the poem, "Annabel Lee":

Passage(s):	Line(s) or Stanza:	Observations, Questions, Literary Device(s)
"**this** maiden she **lived with** no other thought"	Line 3	*This is an example of **Assonance**; the repetition of vowel sounds. Adds a type of undulation or hypnotic quality to the poem.*
"With a love that the winged seraphs of heaven / **Coveted** her and me"	Stanza 11-12	*What does "coveted" mean? What about the angels here?*

Your Turn!

- ✓ Summarize key points.
- ✓ Note repeated words or phrases.
- ✓ Connect ideas
- ✓ What images can you visualize?

© Shake Shock Press
Copyright material

Name: _____

"Annabel Lee"
Activity #26 -- Second Read Note Chart

Second Read Note Chart

Passage(s):	Line(s) or Stanza:	Observations, Questions, Literary Device(s)

Name: _____

"Annabel Lee"
Activity #27 – Vocabulary
All Grade Levels

Directions:

The following vocabulary words are found in the poem. Understanding them will enhance your understanding as you read. Define each one **IN YOUR OWN WORDS** first. Indicate on the chart what context clue(s) you used to help you to determine the meaning. Then, as you read, use a dictionary if needed.

Word	Your definition:	Context Clue(s):
1. Maiden		
2. Winged seraphs		
3. Coveted		
4. Highborn kinsmen		
5. Bore		
6. Sepulchre		
7. Envying		
8. Dissever		
9. Beams		
10. Night-tide		

© Shake Shock Press — Copyright material

Name: _____

"Annabel Lee"
Activity #28: After Reading Questions
Grades 9-10

After Reading Questions

Refer to your charts and to the text directly when you answer the following questions below. You may need to read the poem through several more times to locate key items.

Write your reply to each question below in 2-3 full sentences. Be sure to use proper grammar and punctuation:

1. How long has the speaker known Annabel Lee? How do you know?

2. According to the speaker, how do the angels in heaven feel about his and Annabel Lee's relationship? What do they ultimately do? What line(s) show this?

3. Who else besides the "angels in Heaven" could ever separate the speaker's soul from hers? Give the line here along with your response.

4. What does the speaker say about nature and its connection to his beloved?

5. In the last stanza, the speaker says that he sleeps next to her every night. How is this possible? What, in fact, might this suggest about the speaker?

Name: _____

"Annabel Lee"
Activity #28: After Reading Questions
Grades 11-12

After Reading Questions

Refer to your charts and to the text directly when you answer the following questions below. You may need to read the poem through several more times to locate key items.

Write your responses below in 3-5 full sentences. Be sure to use proper grammar and punctuation as well as evidence from the text, properly cited. Example: (Lines 1-2).

1. How would you describe Annabel Lee based solely on the speaker's words in the poem?

2. What about the speaker? What characteristics stand out to you? Is he mentally stable? What supports this impression?

3. Describe the setting using passages from the text. How does it add to the overall tone and mood created in this poem?

Name: _____ "Annabel Lee"
Activity #29: Podcast Interview Questions
All Grade Levels

Source: Ted.com

Podcast Interview: Edgar Allen Poe

Imagine that you have the opportunity to interview this American poet and short story author of the 19th century as a high school student with your own podcast. Start by first researching his life and perhaps, his motivations for his famous writings and inexplicable, dark persona. Would you have the courage to ask tough questions? Now's your chance!

Write down some of the burning questions that you would have for the esteemed author, Edgar Allen Poe, on a series of note cards like this one here:

Show Name:
Guest: Edgar Allen Poe
Questions:

Name: _____

Poetry Speaks!
Activity #30 – Dramatic Monologue
"My Last Duchess" -- All Grade Levels

Dramatic Monologue

Introduction: A type of poetry that is written in the form of a speech of an individual character. The speaker is not the poet; the speaker interacts with one or more other people in the poem. We are only aware of anything through an invisible "auditor" whose presence affects what the speaker says and how he reacts to the auditor. This technique allows the poet to reveal to the reader the speaker's temperament, character, and motivations in a way in which the reader is "looking on" from a unique vantage point.

Biography: Robert Browning (1812-1889). An English poet and playwright whose dramatic monologues award him high honor among Victorian poets. His writing is often comprised of irony, characterization, dark humor, and commentary on social matters. He typically explored historical settings and wrote in a grammatically distinctive style. In this particular poem and the portrayal of the Duke, Browning critiques the social norms of the Victorian era by presenting sexism and objectification of women as dehumanizing.

Type: Dramatic Monologue. This poem consists of 56 lines in rhyming couplets.

Summary: The narrator of the poem is the Duke of Ferrara (a city in northern Italy). He comments indifferently to an outside observer on a portrait of his late wife hanging on the wall. The duke talks about the duchess's character that the remarks caused him much displeasure due to her friendliness and outgoing nature toward others and her refusal to comply with his superiority in all matters. By the poem's end, it is revealed that it was he, the duke, who caused her untimely death.

© Shake Shock Press   Copyright material

Name: _____

Poetry Speaks!
Activity #30 – Dramatic Monologue
"My Last Duchess" -- All Grade Levels

My Last Duchess
By Robert Browning

That's my last Duchess painted on the wall,
Looking as if she were alive. I call
That piece a wonder, now: Frà Pandolf's hands
Worked busily a day, and there she stands.
Will 't please you sit and look at her? I said
'Frà Pandolf' by design, for never read
Strangers like you that pictured countenance,
The depth and passion of its earnest glance,
But to myself they turned (since none puts by
The curtain I have drawn for you, but I)
And seemed as they would ask me, if they durst,
How such a glance came there; so, not the first
Are you to turn and ask thus. Sir, 't was not
Her husband's presence only, called that spot
Of joy into the Duchess' cheek: perhaps
Frà Pandolf chanced to say, 'Her mantle laps
Over my lady's wrist too much,' or 'Paint
Must never hope to reproduce the faint
Half-flush that dies along her throat:' such stuff
Was courtesy, she thought, and cause enough
For calling up that spot of joy. She had
A heart—how shall I say?—too soon made glad,
Too easily impressed; she liked whate'er
She looked on, and her looks went everywhere.
Sir, 't was all one! My favour at her breast,
The dropping of the daylight in the West,
The bough of cherries some officious fool
Broke in the orchard for her, the white mule
She rode with round the terrace—all and each
Would draw from her alike the approving speech,
Or blush, at least. She thanked men—good! but thanked
Somehow—I know not how—as if she ranked
My gift of a nine-hundred-years-old name
With anybody's gift. Who'd stoop to blame
This sort of trifling? Even had you skill

Poetry Speaks!
Activity #30 – Dramatic Monologue
"My Last Duchess" -- All Grade Levels

In speech—(which I have not)—to make your will
Quite clear to such an one, and say, 'Just this
Or that in you disgusts me; here you miss,
Or there exceed the mark'—and if she let
Herself be lessoned so, nor plainly set
Her wits to yours, forsooth, and made excuse,
—E'en then would be some stooping; and I choose
Never to stoop. Oh, sir, she smiled, no doubt,
Whene'er I passed her; but who passed without
Much the same smile? This grew; I gave commands;
Then all smiles stopped together. There she stands
As if alive. Will 't please you rise? We'll meet
The company below then. I repeat,
The Count your master's known munificence
Is ample warrant that no just pretence
Of mine for dowry will be disallowed;
Though his fair daughter's self, as I avowed
At starting, is my object. Nay, we'll go
Together down, sir. Notice Neptune, though,
Taming a sea-horse, thought a rarity,
Which Claus of Innsbruck cast in bronze for me!

SOURCE: POETS.ORG

SOURCE: EBAY.CO.UK

Name: _____

Poetry Speaks!
Activity #30 – "My Last Duchess"
First Read -- All Grade Levels

The First Read

"My Last Duchess" is one of Robert Browning's later works. He is known for his mastery of the dramatic monologue. His unique style has influenced some of the great poets of the twentieth century. See if you can find these and other literary devices in his unsettling and thought-provoking poem.

Model Chart entries for the poem, "My Last Duchess":

Passage(s):	Line(s) or Stanza:	Observations, Questions, Literary Device(s)
"That's my last Duchess painted on the wall / Looking as if she were alive. I call / That piece a wonder, now; Fra Pandolf's hands / Worked busily a day, and there she stands. / Will't please you sit and look at her?""	Lines 1-5	*The Duke personifies the painting by regarding it as containing a living being. He does not distinguish between a work of art and a living, breathing woman.*
"And seemed as they would ask me, if they durst, / How such a glance came there; so, not the first"	Lines 12-13	*The poem is written in iambic pentameter throughout in rhyming couplets.*

Your Turn!

Use the blank chart on the following page to add your own entries as you read through the poem for the first time. Feel free to make copies of it if you need more space to capture your notes. Some things you might want to take note of:

- ✓ How would you describe the Duke? Are his actions trustworthy?
- ✓ How does he control the conversation? Why might he do this?
- ✓ What does the Duke think about himself? Women in general?

What is your "Likability" Score of this poem (on a scale of 1 to 10 with ten being the highest? ____.

© Shake Shock Press

Name: _____

"My Last Duchess"
Activity #30 -- First Read Note Chart

First Read Note Chart

Passage(s):	Line(s) or Stanza:	Observations, Questions, Literary Device(s)

Name: _____

Poetry Speaks!
Activity #31 – "My Last Duchess"
Second Read – All Grade Levels

The Second Read

Now it's time to read the poem once again, this time, paying special attention to the use of imagery and/or any literary devices used (see **resource list** in the back of this workbook). Once again, you may choose instead to make your notations directly onto the poem. Or, you can use a chart like the one below to help you keep track of your impressions and/or questions.

Model Chart entries for the poem, "My Last Duchess":

Passage(s):	Line(s) or Stanza:	Observations, Questions, Literary Device(s)
"For calling up that spot of joy. She had / A heart—how shall I say?—too soon made glad"	Line 21-22	The rhymes are all perfect rhymes. The scheme is: AABBCCDD
"Sir, 'twas all one! My favour at her breast, / The dropping of the daylight in the West"	Lines 25-26	Iambic pentameter throughout; mimics the sound of regular speech.

Your Turn!

- ✓ Summarize key points.
- ✓ Note repeated words or phrases.
- ✓ Connect ideas
- ✓ What images can you visualize?

Name: _____

"My Last Duchess"
Activity #31 -- Second Read Note Chart

Second Read Note Chart

Passage(s):	Line(s) or Stanza:	Observations, Questions, Literary Device(s)

Name: _____

"My Last Duchess"
Activity #32: Line Analysis
Grades 9-10

Line Analysis

Refer to your charts and to the text directly when you complete the following interpretations below. You may need to read the poem through several more times to locate key meanings. Write your interpretation of the lines given in your own words to translate the meaning.

Example: "Looking as if she were alive. I call / that piece a wonder, now; Fra Pandolf's hands / Worked busily a day, and there she stands."

Interpretation: *The Duke points out how lifelike the painting looks and marvels at what a valuable item it is. He boasts about how hard the artist worked to capture her exact likeness.*

1. "But to myself they turned (since none puts by / The curtain I have drawn for you, but I" (Lines 10-11).

    Interpretation:

2. "Sir, 'twas not / Her husband's presence only, called that spot / Of joy into the Duchess' cheek" (Lines 13-15).

    Interpretation:

3. "She thanked men—good! but thanked / Somehow—I know not how—as if she ranked / My gift of a nine-hundred-years-old name / With anybody's gift" (Lines 31-34).

    Interpretation:

Name: _____

"My Last Duchess"
Activity #32: Line Analysis
Grades 9-10

4. "Oh, sir, she smiled, no doubt, / Whene'er I passed her; but who passed without / Much the same smile? (Lines 43-45).

   Interpretation:

5. "This grew; I gave commands; / Then all smiles stopped together. There she stands / As if alive" (Lines 45-47).

   Interpretation:

6. "Will't please you rise? We'll meet / The company below, then. I repeat / The Count your master's known munificence / Is ample warrant that no just pretense / Of mine for dowry will be disallowed" (Lines 47-51).

   Interpretation:

7. "Though his fair daughter's self, as I avowed / At starting, is my object" (Lines 52-53).

   Interpretation:

8. "Nay, we'll go / Together down, sir. Notice Neptune, though, / Taming a sea-horse, thought a rarity, / Which Claus of Innsbruck cast in bronze for me!" (Lines 53-56).

   Interpretation:

© Shake Shock Press — Copyright material

Name: _____

"My Last Duchess"
Activity #33: Critical Thinking Questions
Grades 9-10

Critical Thinking Questions

Refer to your charts and to the text directly when you answer the following questions below. You may need to read the poem through several more times to locate key meanings.

Write your responses below in 2-3 full sentences. Be sure to use proper grammar and punctuation.

1. To whom is the Duke speaking? Why is this visitor there?

2. According to the Duke, what were the Duchess's "flaws"?

3. In light of the Duke's comments, mannerisms, and demeanor, how would you characterize him?

4. How does the Duke regard women overall? What proof of this can you find in the text?

© Shake Shock Press   Copyright material

Name: _____

"My Last Duchess"
Activity #34: Poem Summary
Grades 11-12

Poem Summary

Refer to your charts and to the text directly when you complete the following activity. You may need to read the poem through several more times to locate key meanings.

Summarize the poem into one paragraph from start to finish. Be sure to use proper grammar and punctuation as well as evidence from the text where able. Be sure to indicate the line number(s) from the poem. Example: (Lines 2-4).

Name: _____

"My Last Duchess"
Activity #34: Poem Summary
Grades 11-12

Name: _____

"My Last Duchess"
Activity #35: Critical Thinking Questions
Grades 11-12

Critical Thinking Questions

Refer to your charts and to the text directly when you answer the following questions below. You may need to read the poem through several more times to locate key meanings.

Write your responses below in 3-5 full sentences. Be sure to use proper grammar and punctuation. Include passages from the text in your responses, properly cited where able. Example: (Lines 2-4).

1. The Duke is showing off a portrait of his late Duchess to the Envoy as the poem opens. What is the **tone** set by the Duke? How does the poet create and maintain this aspect through out the poem?

2. The Duke refers to the artist, Fra Pandolf three times within the first sixteen lines of the poem. What does this indicate?

© Shake Shock Press — Copyright material

Name: _____

"My Last Duchess"
Activity #35: Critical Thinking Questions
Grades 11-12

3. What might the painting itself symbolize in this poem? What greater meaning does it contain to serve as a look into the Duke's psyche?

4. Near the end of the poem, the Duke is delivering a warning to the Envoy, his new potential in-laws, and new wife. What is it?

Name: _____

"My Last Duchess"
Activity #36 – Pick a Persona Journal Writing
All Grades

Pick a Persona – Journal Writing

Choose **ONE** of the personas listed and write in the journal below as the persona listed. Try to capture the tone, dialect, and perspective of the character you are channeling.

The Duchess

Prior to your disappearance, you wrote a letter to your best friend, telling her about your marriage to the Duke. Describe your experiences being his wife from early one and through the time you sat to have your portrait painted. What was life like for you daily? How did you view your life and the people around you? What sorts of things delighted you? What did you think of your husband, the Duke?

Count's Envoy

You are the envoy of the Count, who has sent you to Duke Ferrara to make negotiations for a wedding between the Duke and the Count's daughter. Prior to meeting with his future in-laws and guests, the Duke pulls a curtain aside and reveals a beautiful painting of his former Duchess, whom he begins to describe to you. He tells you to sit while he relays personal information about her flaws and disposition, all of which were displeasing to him. The Duke indicates that he had her killed because she was not attentive to him fully. Based on this knowledge, what kind of life can the Count's daughter expect as the new Duchess? Would you recommend that she marry the Duke? What are your reasons? Use the Duke's own words to make your argument to the Count.

Brother Pandolf

You are brother Pandolf, a man of the cloth, who painted the portrait of the Duchess. You keep a journal where you write down your thoughts about all of your paintings and the people and experiences that shaped their creation. You have seen a lot during the time that you spent at the mansion. You have decided to write your account and your feelings about the Duchess and her husband, the Duke of Ferrara. Based on your knowledge of events, describe the Duchess, the Duke, and their relationship.

© Shake Shock Press — Copyright material

Name: _____

"My Last Duchess"
Activity #36 – Pick a Persona Journal Writing
All Grades

Name: _____

"My Last Duchess"
Activity #36 – Pick a Persona Journal Writing
All Grades

Poetry Speaks!
Activity #37: -- Concrete Poems
All Grades

Concrete Poems

Definition: Concrete poems are a visual arrangement of text, images, and/or symbols, usually shaped or patterned in some way. The words and how they appear on the page depict the subject matter, or complement the theme, symbol, or main idea. It's as simple as that! Take a look at some examples.

SOURCE: POEMSEARCHER.COM

Name: _____

Poetry Speaks!
Activity #37: -- Concrete Poems
All Grades

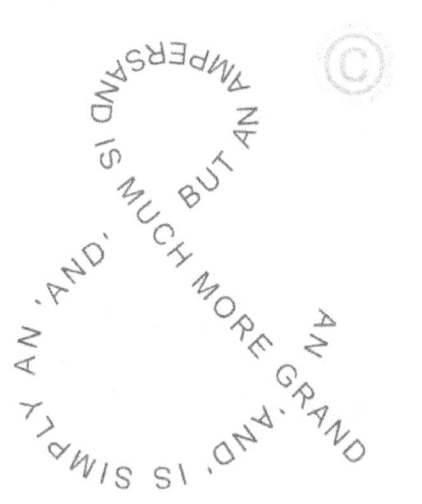

Source: Slideserve.com

Source: sites.google.com

Source: sites.google.com

Name: _____

Poetry Speaks!
Activity #37: -- Concrete Poems
All Grades

Source: freewordcloudgenerator.com

Source: Pinterest.com

© Shake Shock Press — Copyright material

Name: _____
Poetry Speaks!
Activity #37: Create Your Own Concrete Poem
All Grades

Your Turn!

Now it's time for you to try your hand at creating a concrete poem! Works of concrete poetry are as much works of visual art, as they are poems. Think of a topic and have some fun with this! Sketch your work here below for a keepsake of your own masterpiece.

Photos/screenshots are welcome if you want a chance to publish your work on my social media page at www.jamiecollinsteacher.com.

Place your concrete poem in the frame on the next page:

```
                                    Bowin
                                    into th
                              dojo, I
                                empty all
                                my thoughts
                               and focus solely
                      on     karate. The
                          word,    karate, means
      "empty         hand" or hand     "empty of
      emotions."     To start the class,   we recite three
words: Kigan,  which stands for peace,   Kaishu, which stands
for optimism, and Hoken, which stands for  humility. These are
words that martial artists have        committed to live by.
      As a black belt, I have       experienced first hand
      how much perseverance   and commitment it
      takes. From perfecting a form to advancing
      a new belt rank, you must have the proper
      mindset. Even though you are sore, sweaty,
      or tired, you must keep going. Karate has
      taught me self-discipline, not just in
          the dojo, but at home and at school. It is
          not just about      fighting, but also
            about living a    positive, proactive
                  life.     At the end of
                      class, everyday,
                      we recite the
                      Principles of
                      Black Belt:
                      modesty, courtesy,
                      integrity,
                      perseverance,
                      courage, and
                      indomitable
                        spirit.
                        Karate
                         is more
                         than a
                         sport; it
                    is lifestyle.
```

SOURCE: TUMBLR.COM

Name: _____

Poetry Speaks!
Activity #37: Create Your Own Concrete Poem

Name: _____

Poetry Speaks!
Activity #38 – Haiku Poetry
All Grade Levels

Haiku

Introduction/Background: Haiku is a type of short form, unrhymed poetry that originates from 17th century Japan. Traditional Japanese haiku consist of seventeen syllables arranged in three lines of 5, 7, and 5 syllables (sometimes lost in translation when converted to English syllables). Its themes often focus on images from nature. It presents a focus on a single moment in time, offers the ability to read in one breath, and delivers a type of enlightenment and/or delight. The Haiku is the epitome of simplicity, strength, and truthfulness of expression.

Type: Short form verse

Theme: Nature and/or seasonal.

Traditional forms:

Haiku

By Matsuo Basho (1644-1694)

An old silent pond…
A frog jumps into the pond,
Splash! Silence again.

SOURCE: SHIAPENGLISH.BLOGSPOT.COM

Haiku

By Yosa Bunson (1716-1784)

A summer river being crossed
how pleasing
with sandals in my hands!

SOURCE: TEENINK.COM

© Shake Shock Press — Copyright material

Name: _____

Poetry Speaks!
Activity #38 – Haiku Poetry
All Grade Levels

Modern forms:

Haiku [for you]
By Sonia Sanchez (1934 -)

love between us is
speech and breath. Loving you is
a long river running.

SOURCE: POETS.ORG

Haiku (Spring)

Sloppy puddles. Wet.
My dog's feet, tracking muddy
Paw prints on my floor.

SOURCE: CLASSROOMPOEMS.COM

Haiku (Summer)

I feel the sun's warmth
Baking on my skin. I watch
The flowers reach high.

SOURCE: CLASSROOMPOEMS.COM

Name: _____ Poetry Speaks!
Activity #38 – Write Your Own Haiku Poetry
All Grade Levels

Your Turn!

Are you ready to give this ancient poetic form a try? In keeping with the 5, 7, 5 syllable structure (three lines), try your hand at writing your own haiku poems about the following topics:

Haiku (Fall)

By _____

1.

2.

3.

Haiku (Winter)

By _____

1.

2.

3.

© Shake Shock Press · Copyright material

Name: _____   Poetry Speaks!
Activity #38 – Write Your Own Haiku Poetry
All Grade Levels

Haiku (A pet)

By _____

1.

2.

3.

Haiku (Being a teen)

By _____

1.

2.

3.

Name: _____

Poetry Speaks!
Activity #39 – Free Verse
All Grade Levels

Free Verse

Introduction: Free Verse is an open form of poetry. Such poems do not use consistent meter, rhyme, or any musical pattern. In other words, it is poetry that does not rhyme or have a regular rhythm. Note: This does not mean that the poet can *never* use meter or rhyme. The poet is free to include these elements if he or she chooses. As there is no restriction on the length of lines, use of stanzas, and/or the way in which words are broken up/arranged, the poet has control over this as well.

Background: Although the author, Walt Whitman is said to be the father of free verse by popularizing this poetic form, many poets before him also wrote in this free-style way. Robert Frost once called it, "Playing tennis without a net."

Type: No types or forms—free of formal constraints.

Song of America
By Jamie Collins

Oh, brother,
Oh, sister –
How can I put into words what
I am seeing, feeling, fearing?
Comfort and *Mercy* gliding on our ravished shores,
Lady Liberty, watchmen of all we hold dear;
Who heralds freedom, hope, and might,
Seems to shed a thousand tears;
City rising from the scourge.

What sense is there in empty words--
Shelves, streets, and halls?
What madness has replaced the hum
Of life in all her glorious beats,

Name: _____

Poetry Speaks!
Activity #39 – Free Verse
All Grade Levels

Resounding now with crushing chaos,
Daily blows of shock and grief?

Oh, brother,
Oh, sister –
What is this dream?
How to sort the when's and why's?
What rise do we by fate or grace
Above this gruesome test?
Still, to give and find in ourselves
The very worst; the very best.

Called are we to close our doors,
To shutter not our hearts, but to wait.
With sorrow, fear, and pain
As the hands and hearts of masked angels
Work to heal and toil in vain.

Oh, brother,
Oh, sister –
In this harrowing hour,
Hold fast, rise up, be strong!
See in our fragility the hidden power.

And to He who counts our days and hours
Measure out life's joyful songs,
In spite of the madness and searing desperation.
Bring us rescue, breath, and valor.
Bring us to the light.

SOURCE: SHAKE SHOCK PRESS

Name: _____

Poetry Speaks!
Activity #39 – "Song of America"
First Read -- All Grade Levels

The First Read

"Song of America" is a poem written by Jamie Collins, a teacher and American author. Written in 2020, this poem was in response to the turmoil of the COVID pandemic, namely its wrath upon the city of New York as a gateway to the nation and the world. It relays the fear and uncertainty at a time when everything changed in everyday life save for the unbending strength of a people, a city, and a nation rooted in faith. It is an anthem of hope in a time of strife.

Model Chart entries for the poem, "Song of America":

Passage(s):	Line(s) or Stanza:	Observations, Questions, Literary Device(s)
"Song of America"	Title	*This gives the impression that the poem will have some lyrical elements even though it is written in free verse.*
"*Comfort* and *Mercy* gliding on our ravished shores"	Line 5	*Refers to the military ships used as floating hospitals during the pandemic.*

Your Turn!

Use the blank chart on the following page to add your own entries as you read through the poem for the first time. Feel free to make copies of it if you need more space to capture your notes. Some things you might want to take note of:

- ✓ What is the feeling evoked in the poem overall?
- ✓ How does the author use literary devices to convey a sense of both fear and strength?
- ✓ What is the underlying message of this poem?

What is your "Likability" Score of this poem (on a scale of 1 to 10 with ten being the highest? ____.

Name: _____

"Song of America"
Activity #39 -- First Read Note Chart

First Read Note Chart

Passage(s):	Line(s) or Stanza:	Observations, Questions, Literary Device(s)

Name: _____

Poetry Speaks!
Activity #40 – "Song of America"
Second Read – All Grade Levels

The Second Read

Now it's time to read the poem once again, this time, paying special attention to the use of imagery and/or any literary devices used (see **resource list** in the back of this workbook). Once again, you may choose instead to make your notations directly onto the poem. Or, you can use a chart like the one below to help you keep track of your impressions and/or questions.

Model Chart entries for the poem, "Song of America":

Passage(s):	Line(s) or Stanza:	Observations, Questions, Literary Device(s)
"Lady Liberty, watchmen of all we hold dear; / Who heralds freedom, hope, and might, / Seems to shed a thousand tears"	Lines 6-8	**Personification** of the Statue of Liberty, actually crying for the people stricken with the virus.
"As the hands and hearts of masked angels"	Line 27	A **metaphor** describing the doctors and nurses tending to the COVID patients as being angels.

Your Turn!

✓ Summarize key points.
✓ Note repeated words or phrases.
✓ Connect ideas
✓ What images can you visualize?

© Shake Shock Press   Copyright material

Name: _____

"Song of America"
Activity #40 -- Second Read Note Chart

Second Read Note Chart

Passage(s):	Line(s) or Stanza:	Observations, Questions, Literary Device(s)

© Shake Shock Press — Copyright material

Name: _____

"Song of America"
Activity #41: Short Answer Questions
Grades 9-10

Short Answer Questions

Refer to your charts and to the text directly when you answer the following questions below. You may need to read the poem through several more times to locate key meanings.

Write your responses below in 2-3 full sentences. Be sure to use proper grammar and punctuation.

1. To whom is the speaker addressing? How is the message enhanced by the use of words, "Brother" and "Sister"?

2. What is the "crushing chaos" in the streets, shelves, and halls?

3. In stanza five, the speaker says, "Called are we to close our doors, / To shutter not our hearts, but to wait". What does this mean in light of the pandemic at the time?

4. In stanza 6, what is the speaker asking his or her brothers and sisters to do?

5. Who does the speaker appeal to in the final stanza? Why?

© Shake Shock Press — Copyright material

Name: _____

"Song of America"
Activity #42: After Reading Questions
Grades 11-12

After Reading Questions

Refer to your charts and to the text directly when you answer the following questions below. You may need to read the poem through several more times to locate key items.

Write your responses below in 3-5 full sentences. Be sure to use proper grammar and punctuation as well as evidence from the text, properly cited. Example: (Lines 1-2).

1. How would you describe the speaker's *tone* at the beginning of the poem as opposed to the end?

2. How does the poem's *form* contribute to the impact and/or the message?

3. What is the "gruesome test"? How does the speaker regard America's chance to withstand it?

© Shake Shock Press — Copyright material

Name: _____

"Poetry Speaks!"
Activity #43: Pre-Writing Exercise
All Grades

Write Your Own Free Verse Poem

Do you have an idea for a free verse poem of your own? How can you take something from your life and turn it into a thoughtful expression that you can share with the world? Or, if you would rather not share it, your poem can just be a personal addition to your journal to look back on someday.

Prompt: Write your own free verse poem about being a teen. Be sure to use one or more of the literary terms and techniques that you have learned.

Use this space for your brainstorming and prewriting ideas first:

Name: _____

"Poetry Speaks!"
Activity #44: Writing Exercise
All Grades

Write Your Free Verse Poem

[Title]
By [Your Name]

Name: _____

Poetry Speaks!
Activity #45: Poetry Exam – Grades 9-10

Poetry Exam (Grades 9-10)

Hopefully, you are ready to test your knowledge of what you have learned about both classic as well as modern poetry. Use this workbook as a resource to complete this exam.

*Choose the best answer below, and write the corresponding letter in the blank.

1. Which is **NOT** a form of figurative language?
    a. simile
    b. glossaries
    c. imagery
    d. metaphor

2. **Alliteration** is
    a. repetition of beginning consonant sounds   in a group of words
    b. repetition of vowel sounds at the beginning, middle, or end of a word
    c. a reference to something else
    d. rhythmic form in a poem

3. **Form** in poetry refers to
    a. a word's second meaning
    b. the structure or shape of a written work
    c. a repetition of sounds
    d. an exact rhyme

Name: _____   Poetry Speaks!
Activity #45: Poetry Exam – Grades 9-10

4. **Tone** is defined as

    a. the emotional coloring of the work (angry, sad, joyful, ominous)

    b. repetitive sounds of end rhymes part of the stressed syllable

    c. the pitch of a poet's voice

    d. the highest part of the stressed syllable

5. A term for words that *sound like* what they mean is

    a. onomatopoeia

    b. understatement

    c. oxymoron

    d. hyperbole

6. **Meter** in poetry is defined as

    a. a British yardstick

    b. the number of feet within a line of traditional verse

    c. free-form verse

    d. the distance a poet can travel in one hour

7. An **end-stopped** line is

    a. a line of poetry that has no punctuation and runs into the next line

    b. a period or semicolon at the end of a line of verse

    c. a line of poetry ending in a full pause

    d. b & c

Name: _____   Poetry Speaks!
Activity #45: Poetry Exam – Grades 9-10

8. Which of the following are examples of strategies used to assess a poem for the first reading?

    a. read it through and take a "gut check"

    b. observe the punctuation and form

    c. predict the meaning based on the title

    d. all of the above

9. *"And yet, by heaven, I think my love as real / As any she believed with false compare"* is an excerpt from

    a. a. Ode on a Grecian Urn

    b. Ego Tripping

    c. Annabel Lee

    d. Sonnet 130

10. The **three main poetic forms** that were examined in this workbook were:

    a. _____

    b. _____

    c. _____

*Answer the following statements as either True or False

11. Stanza is a division in poetry equivalent to a paragraph in prose. T/F

12. Words that trigger a picture in the reader's mind of visual and sensory images is referred to as **imagery**. T/F

13. An example of **hyperbole** is, "bright night" when the poet is referring to the starry sky. T/F

Name: _____ Poetry Speaks!
Activity #45: Poetry Exam – Grades 9-10

14. Always use "quotation marks" when writing the title of a poem. T/F

15. An example if **metaphor** is, *"Juliet is the sun."* T/F

16. A meter refers to the number of feet within a line of traditional verse, such as iambic pentameter. T/F

***Match the correct terms**

17. *I think that I shall never see*
    A poem as lovely as a tree

    a. couplet

    b. quatrain

    c. sestet

    d. octave

18. What is the rhyme scheme of a Shakespearean sonnet:

    a. ABA ABA CD

    b. ABAB CDCD EFEF GG

    c. EKG EKG ZZ

    d. CDCM CDCM

19. "*Once upon a midnight **dreary**, while I pondered, weak and **weary***" is an example of:

    a. run-on line

    b. internal rhyme

    c. sonnet

    d. end-stopped line

Name: _____

Poetry Speaks!
Activity #45: Poetry Exam – Grades 9-10

*Read the excerpt from "Song of the Open Road" by Walt Whitman. Use what you notice about the poetic elements to determine the tone.

Excerpt from

"Song of the Open Road"
by Walt Whitman

Afoot and lighthearted I take the open road.

Healthy, free, the world before me leading wherever I choose.

Henceforth I ask not good-fortune, I myself am good-fortune.

Henceforth, I whimper no more, postpone no more, need nothing,

5   Done with indoor complaints, libraries, querulous criticisms.

Strong and content I travel the open road.

Source: poemanalysis.com

20. What is this poem mainly about?

   a. The speaker has decided to stop complaining about life.

   b. The speaker feels he has spent too much time indoors.

   c. The speaker has recently recovered from an illness and is taking a trip.

   d. The speaker has a new, confident outlook on life and feels adventurous.

Name: _____

Poetry Speaks!
Activity #45: Poetry Exam – Grades 9-10

21. What does the reader learn in the opening stanza to this poem?
Summarize the excerpt, line by line, in *your own* words.

Name: _____

Poetry Speaks!
Activity #45: Poetry Exam – Grades 9-10

22. What is the **tone** of this poem?

    a. optimistic

    b. defensive

    c. informal

    d. angry

23. What does the tone reveal about how the speaker <u>feels</u> about setting off on a new path?

    a. The speaker is anxious to return to his normal life.

    b. The speaker is excited and a little nervous.

    c. The speaker is confident and happy.

    d. The speaker is hasty are careless.

24. Who is the author of this poem?

    a. Robert Frost

    b. e e cummings

    c. Walt Whitman

    d. Shakespeare

Name: _____

Poetry Speaks!
Activity #45: Poetry Exam – Grades 9-10

Match the definitions with the literary terms from the word bank below:

Definition:	Literary Term:
25. A visual arrangement of text, images, and/or symbols shaped or patterned that makes up a poem.	
26. An open form of poetry that does not use consistent meter, rhyme, or any musical pattern.	
27. A type of poetry that is written in the form of a speech of an individual character.	
28. Short-form, unrhymed poetry that originated in Japan; 17 syllables arranged in three lines of 5, 7, 5, respectively.	
29. A form of poetry that tells a story through verse.	
30. A type of poetry that utilizes words and phrases similar to current music/rap lyrics.	
31. A serious or thoughtful poem that is written to pay homage to someone or something.	

Free Verse   **Narrative**   **Concrete Poem**

Haiku   **Dramatic monologue**   **Hip Hop**

Ode

Name: _____

Poetry Speaks!
Activity #46: Poetry Exam – Grades 11-12

Poetry Exam (Grades 11-12)

Hopefully, you are ready to test your knowledge of what you have learned about both classic as well as modern poetry. Use this workbook as a resource to complete this exam.

*Choose the best answer below, and write the corresponding letter in the blank.

1. Which is **NOT** a form of figurative language?

    a. simile

    b. glossaries

    c. imagery

    d. metaphor

2. **Alliteration** is

    a. repetition of beginning consonant sounds in a group of words

    b. repetition of vowel sounds at the beginning, middle, or end of a word

    c. a reference to something else

    d. rhythmic form in a poem

3. **Form** in poetry refers to

    a. a word's second meaning

    b. the structure or shape of a written work

    c. a repetition of sounds

    d. an exact rhyme

Name: _____   Poetry Speaks!
Activity #46: Poetry Exam – Grades 11-12

4. **Tone** is defined as

    a. the emotional coloring of the work voice

    b. repetitive sounds of end rhymes part of the stressed syllable

    c. the pitch of a poet's voice (angry, sad, joyful, ominous)

    d. the highest part of the stressed syllable

5. A term for words that *sound like* what they mean is

    a. onomatopoeia

    b. understatement

    c. oxymoron

    d. hyperbole

6. **Meter** in poetry is defined as

    a. a British yardstick

    b. the number of feet within a line of traditional verse

    c. free-form verse

    d. the distance a poet can travel in one hour

7. An **end-stopped** line is

    a. a line of poetry that has no punctuation and runs into the next line

    b. a period or semicolon at the end of a line of verse

    c. a line of poetry ending in a full pause

    d. b & c

Name: _____   Poetry Speaks!
                                                Activity #46: Poetry Exam – Grades 11-12

8. Which of the following are examples of strategies used to assess a poem for the first reading?

   a. read it through and take a "gut check"

   b. observe the punctuation and form

   c. predict the meaning based on the title

   d. all of the above

9. *"And yet, by heaven, I think my love as real / As any she believed with false compare"* is an excerpt from

   a. Ode on a Grecian Urn

   b. Ego Tripping

   c. Annabel Lee

   d. Sonnet 130

10. The **three main poetic forms** that were examined in this workbook were:

    a. _____

    b. _____

    c. _____

*Answer the following statements as either True or False

11. Stanza is a division in poetry equivalent to a paragraph in prose. T/F

12. Words that trigger a picture in the reader's mind of visual and sensory images is referred to as **imagery**. T/F

13. An example of **hyperbole** is, "bright night" when the poet is referring to the starry sky. T/F

Name: _____   Poetry Speaks!
Activity #46: Poetry Exam – Grades 11-12

14. Always use "quotation marks" when writing the title of a poem. T/F

15. An example if **metaphor** is, *"Juliet is the sun."* T/F

16. A meter refers to the number of feet within a line of traditional verse, such as iambic pentameter. T/F

***Match the correct terms**

17. *I think that I shall never see*
    A poem as lovely as a tree

    a. couplet

    b. quatrain

    c. sestet

    d. octave

18. What is the rhyme scheme of a Shakespearean sonnet:

    a. ABA ABA CD

    b. ABAB CDCD EFEF GG

    c. EKG EKG ZZ

    d. CDCM CDCM

19. *"Once upon a midnight **dreary**, while I pondered, weak and **weary**"* …is an example of:

    a. run-on line

    b. internal rhyme

    c. sonnet

    d. end-stopped line

Name: _____   Poetry Speaks!
                                                Activity #46: Poetry Exam – Grades 11-12

*Read the following poem. Use what you notice about the poetic elements to determine the tone.

"Taking Leave of a Friend"
Version by Ezra Pound

Blue mountains to the north of the walls,

White river winding about them;

Here we must make a separation

And go out through a thousand miles

5   of dead grass.

Mind like a floating wide cloud,

Sunset like the parting of old acquaintances

Who bow over their clasped hands at a distance.

Our horses neigh to each other

10   as we are departing.

SOURCE: POEMHUNTER.COM

20. What is the subject of this poem?

    a. love

    b. nature

    c. parting

    d. friendship

Name: _____ Poetry Speaks!
Activity #46: Poetry Exam – Grades 11-12

21. Which of these images provides a clue about the season?

    a. white river

    b. dead grass

    c. blue mountains

    d. floating wide cloud

22. Line 6 is an example of:

    a. metaphor

    b. onomatopoeia

    c. simile

    d. personification

23. Do you think that the poet's comparison between the sunset and old acquaintances clasping each other's hands and bowing before departing is effective? What do these two things have in common? Give your analysis. Be sure to include the line number(s).

_____

_____

_____

_____

_____

_____

_____

© Shake Shock Press   Copyright material

Name: _____

Poetry Speaks!
Activity #46: Poetry Exam – Grades 11-12

Name: _____   Poetry Speaks!
Activity #46: Poetry Exam – Grades 11-12

Write the correct poem *type* for each definition:

Definition:	Literary Term:
24. A visual arrangement of text, images, and/or symbols shaped or patterned that makes up a poem.	
25. An open form of poetry that does not use consistent meter, rhyme, or any musical pattern.	
26. A type of poetry that is written in the form of a speech of an individual character.	
27. Short-form, unrhymed poetry that originated in Japan; 17 syllables arranged in three lines of 5, 7, 5, respectively.	
28. A form of poetry that tells a story through verse.	
29. A type of poetry that utilizes words and phrases similar to current music/rap lyrics.	
30. A serious or thoughtful poem that is written to pay homage to someone or something.	
31. A fourteen-line poem written in iambic pentameer.	

© Shake Shock Press   Copyright material

Name: _____

Poetry Speaks!
Activity #46: Poetry Exam – Grades 11-12

"The Red Wheelbarrow"
by William Carlos Williams

1   So much depends

2   upon

3   a red wheel

4   barrow

5   glazed with rain

6   water

7   beside the white

8   chickens

SOURCE: POETRYFOUNDATION.ORG

32. This poem best depicts what?

    a. tone

    b. metaphor

    c. imagery

    d. plot

33. How does the poet convey a vivid, precise picture in the reader's mind?

    a. by use of theme

    b. clever characterization

    c. by creating a sense of suspense

    d. uses language effectively to paint a picture

© Shake Shock Press   Copyright material

Name: _____ Poetry Speaks!
Activity #46: Poetry Exam – Grades 11-12

34. What form of poetry is "The Red Wheelbarrow"?

   a. narrative

   b. free verse

   c. lyric

   d. elegy

35. What might the wheelbarrow **symbolize** in this poem?

_____

_____

_____

_____

_____

36. How does the **form** of the poem add to one's understanding?

_____

_____

_____

_____

_____

Name: _____

Poetry Speaks!
Activity #46: Poetry Exam – Grades 11-12

37. What is the theme of the poem, "The Red Wheelbarrow"? Chose from, "Idealization of an everyday object," "Agriculture and society," or "The value of simplicity." Choose one and write a well-formed paragraph. Be sure to include the line number(s) with your analysis.

Name: _____

Poetry Speaks!
Activity #46: Poetry Exam – Grades 11-12

Name: _____

Poetry Speaks!
Activity #46: Poetry Exam – Grades 11-12

Background: This poem by Jamaican-American author, Claude McKay was first published in 1921. He is a noted figure of the Harlem Renaissance era, having moved to New York City at age 25 where he lived in Harlem, a historically Black neighborhood in the 1920s. The poem conveys his uncertain and not always glowing feelings toward America.

"America"
by Claude McKay

Although she feeds me bread of bitterness,

And sinks into my throat her tiger's tooth,

Stealing my breath of life, I will confess

I love this cultured hell that tests my youth.

5   Her vigor flows like tides into my blood,

Giving me strength erect against her hate,

Her bigness sweeps my being like a flood.

Yet, as a rebel fronts a king in state,

I stand within her walls with not a shred

10   Of terror, malice, not a word of jeer.

Darkly I gaze into the days ahead,

And see her might and granite wonders there,

Beneath the touch of Time's unerring hand,

Like priceless treasures sinking in the sand.

SOURCE: POETRYFOUNDATION.ORG

Name: _____

Poetry Speaks!
Activity #46: Poetry Exam – Grades 11-12

38. The poetic device highlighted here is called what? *"Although she feeds me **b**read of **b**itterness, / And sinks into my **t**hroat her **t**iger's **t**ooth"*

    a. tone

    b. alliteration

    c. imagery

    d. plotting

39. The lines, "***she** feeds me,*" "***Her** vigor flows like tides*" and "***Her** bigness sweeps my being like flood,*" assign a human quality to America. This is called what?

    a. metaphor

    b. hyperbole

    c. personification

    d. ballad

40. The type of rhyme that occurs in lines 10 and 12 in the words "jeer" and "there" is called what?

    a. slant rhyme

    b. masculine rhyme

    c. double rhyme

    d. hard rhyme

41. This poem is a sonnet written in iambic pentameter. The rhyme scheme is that of an English sonnet, which is

    a. ABC ABC DD EE GG

    b. ABAB CDCD EFEF GG

    c. CDCD CDCD CM CM

    d. ABAB CDCD EFG EFG

© Shake Shock Press   Copyright material

Name: _____

Poetry Speaks!
Activity #46: Poetry Exam – Grades 11-12

42. Summarize the poem in one short paragraph in **plain language** as if you were the speaker.

_____
_____
_____
_____
_____
_____
_____

43. Discuss the theme of both "resentment and love" that exist in the speaker toward his America. Be sure to include proper in-text citations in your response.

_____
_____
_____
_____
_____
_____
_____

Name: _____

Poetry Speaks!
Activity #46: Poetry Exam – Grades 11-12

44. How does this poem, "America" compare to the overall message found in, "Song of America," which you read in the free verse section? In what ways are the two poems similar? How are they different? Respond in a well thought out paragraph with proper punctuation, grammar, and in-text citations from both works included in your analysis.

_____

_____

_____

_____

_____

_____

_____

_____

_____

_____

_____

_____

_____

_____

Name: _____

Poetry Speaks!
Free-form Journal Writing

Additional Templates & Forms:
Journal Writing

© Shake Shock Press · Copyright material

Name: _____

Poetry Speaks!
First Read Note Chart

First Read Note Chart

Passage(s):	Line(s) or Stanza:	Observations, Questions, Literary Device(s)

© Shake Shock Press — Copyright material

Name: _____

Poetry Speaks!
Second Read Note Chart

Second Read Note Chart

Passage(s):	Line(s) or Stanza:	Observations, Questions, Literary Device(s)

Literary Terms
Poetic Language – Fill in Study Guide

1. alliteration: _____

Example:

2. assonance: _____

Example:

3. consonance: _____

Example:

4. form: _____

Example:

5. onomatopoeia: _____

Example:

6. parallelism: _____

Example:

7. repetition: _____

Example:

8. refrain: _____

Example:

9. rhythm: _____

Example:

10. run-on lines: _____

Example:

11. end-stopped lines: _____

Example:

12. stanza: _____

Example:

13. poetic license: _____

Example:

14. symbol: _____

Example:

15. tone: _____

Example:

16. metaphor: _____

Example:

17. simile: _____

Example:

18. personification: _____

Example:

19. allusion: _____

Example:

20. hyperbole: _____

Example:

You Did It!

Congratulations! You have come to the end of the **Poetry Speaks! Workbook** and have completed all of the assignments. You are now officially a **Poetry Speaks!** High School Scholar and can feel confident that you know how to read, interpret, and analyze different forms of poetry that you might encounter in everyday life, or in higher learning. At best, this journey has made you far more proficient in understanding some notable forms of both traditional as well as contemporary poetry. This is a wonderful and creative literary gift that you have given yourself!

Great job!

Certificate of Completion

Shake Shock Press gives

_____

this award for stellar performance
in the completion of the **Poetry Speaks!**
Student Workbook.

_____   _____
JAMIE COLLINS   **SHAKE SHOCK PRESS**
Author / Teacher   Publisher

Answer Key

Activity #1 – Quick Starter Quiz: (1) Answers may vary. Some responses might include: Haiku, Ballad, Ode, Couplet, Elegy, Sonnet, and/or Concrete poem. (2) Answers may vary. Some responses might include: William Shakespeare, Langston Hughes, Emily Dickinson, Robert Browning, Elizabeth Barrett Browning. Robert Frost, E E Cummings, T S Elliott, Walt Whitman, Edgar Allan Poe, Sylvia Plath, Maya Angelou and/or Dr. Seuss. (3) True. (4) Responses might include: alliteration, diction, dramatic monologue, hyperbole, metaphor, personification, refrain, rhyme, simile, and/or stanza. (This is a partial list). (5). Three lines – c. (6). Dramatic. (7) Responses will vary. (8). No. BONUS QUESTIONS: Answers will vary.

Activity #2 – Free Write (All Levels): Responses will vary.

Activity #3 – "Locker Riot" - First Read (All Levels): Student is to complete the worksheet "First Read Note Chart" adding notes, line number(s), rhyme scheme labels, and/or reactions to the text. Can write directly in the workbook, or print out additional charts from the templates located at the back of the workbook. A minimum of seven entries is suggested.

Activity #4 – "Locker Riot" - Second Read (All Levels): Student is to complete the worksheet "Second Read Note Chart" adding key points, questions, identification of literary devices, and/or new reactions to the text. Can write directly in the workbook, or print out additional charts from the templates located at the back of the workbook. A minimum of seven entries is suggested.

Activity #5 – "Sonnet 130" – First Read (All Levels): Student is to complete the worksheet "First Read Note Chart" adding notes, line number(s), rhyme scheme labels, and/or reactions to the text. Can write directly in the workbook, or print out additional charts from the templates located at the back of the workbook. A minimum of seven entries is suggested.

My mistress' eyes are nothing like the sun; **A**
Coral is far more red than her lips' red; **B**
If snow be white, why then her breasts are dun; **A**
If hairs be wires, black wires grow on her head. **B**
I have seen roses damasked, red and white, **C**
But no such roses see I in her cheeks; **D**
And in some perfumes is there more delight **C**
Than in the breath that from my mistress reeks. **D**
I love to hear her speak, yet well I know **E**
That music hath a far more pleasing sound; **F**
I grant I never saw a goddess go; **E**
My mistress, when she walks, treads on the ground. **F**
And yet, by heaven, I think my love as rare **G**
As any she belied with false compare. **G**

Activity #6 – "Sonnet 130" – Second Read (All Levels): Student is to complete the worksheet "Second Read Note Chart" adding key points, questions, identification of literary devices, and/or new reactions to the text. Can write directly in the workbook, or print out additional charts from the templates located at the back of the workbook. A minimum of seven entries is suggested.

Activity #7 – After Reading Questions (Grades 9-10): (1) True, (2) True, (3) False, (4) False, (5) True, (6) *My mistress' eyes are not beautiful like the sun; coral is far redder than her lips are red. If snow is white, her breasts by comparison are a brownish grey color. If hairs could be likened to wires, she has black wires growing on her head. I know the colors that hue different roses, and none of the brilliance glows in her cheeks. The pleasure from some perfumes is far more appealing than my mistress' fowl breath. I enjoy her voice, but music is far more pleasing. It is true that I have never actually seen a goddess walking by; as for my mistress, she is firmly planted to the ground when she walks. In spite of all of this, by heaven's word, my mistress and my love for her is real and not a design of other poets' imagination.*

Activity #7 – After Reading Questions (Grades 11-12): (1) "If snow be white, why then her breasts are dun;" (Line 3). (2) Shakespeare suggests that love and beauty should not be understood through abstract comparisons, but rather should be valued for being real and flawed. This is true love. (3) Physical attributes are superficial; even though love and beauty are inherently imperfect, they are still something of great worth. Here, Shakespeare is very likely satirizing the concept of contemporary (of his time), love poems. (4) The speaker is saying that he does not mean to degrade his mistress, but to only point out that no one possesses ethereal beauty or does not have flaws. That in the end, such comparisons are not the best way to relay thoughts about love or beauty.

Activity #8 – Create a Sonnet (All Grades): Students should choose one of the themes listed to write their own 14-line sonnet in Shakespeare rhyming scheme. Can be in Old English or modern day vernacular. Responses will vary.

Activity #9 – "Ego Tripping" – First Read (All Levels): Student is to complete the worksheet "First Read Note Chart" adding notes, line number(s), questions, and/or reactions to the text. Can write directly in the workbook, or print out additional charts from the templates located at the back of the workbook. A minimum of seven entries is suggested.

Activity #10 – "Ego Tripping" – Second Read (All Levels): Student is to complete the worksheet "Second Read Note Chart" adding key points, questions, identification of literary devices, and/or new reactions to the text. Can write directly in the workbook, or print out additional charts from the templates located at the back of the workbook. A minimum of seven entries is suggested.

Activity #11 – After Reading Questions (Grades 9-10): (1) The title "Ego-Tripping," can suggest many things: an act or course of action that enhances and satisfies one's ego, a celebration of pride, acting "crazy" or having your mind blown, such as in experiencing something hard to believe or take in. (2) The "I" in the poem is the creator or all things; a deity; God. The speaker is taking credit for supernatural elements such as the beginning of time, the creation of Egyptian marvels, deserts, civilizations, and a metamorphosis into Christ, etc. (3) "sowing diamonds," "created the Nile," "crossing the desert in three hours," etc. (4) It creates momentum and emphasizes the speaker's self-praise for overcoming unfair challenges. (5) Answers will vary. Students might connect the aspect of empowerment, tradition, and endurance of black females throughout history, coming to light in the present day with focus on gender and racial equality.

Activity #11 – After Reading Questions (Grades 11-12): (1) The speaker is said to have, "turned myself into myself and was / Jesus" (Lines 30-31), Her sons are named as Hannibal and Noah, and she creates resources such as "diamonds" (Line 35), and "uranium" (Line 36) as her gifts to humankind. Her conclusion speaks to her divine perfection and female strength and successes, by saying that "even my errors are correct: (Line 42). She attests that her state of perfectionism is beyond comprehension. (2) "I walk to the Fertile Crescent and built the Sphinx" (Lines 2-3) imitates the movement of the speaker (walking for seven long syllables), and the two stressed syllables "built" and "sphinx" complete the task of creation quickly, emphasizing the power of the god-like action of building the sphinx. There is a rhyme pattern in "so ethereal so surreal" (Line 47) that works to create a fluidity that moves the poem forward. The poem's varying rhythms create a sort of improvisational jazz "feel" and sound when spoken out loud. (3) The building of the "Sphinx" (Line 3), "I designed a pyramid" (Line 4), "My oldest daughter is Nefertiti" (Line 12), "Created the Nile" (Line 14). (4) The empowered tone in Giovanni's poem is so prevailing due to the tragic history of African Slavery. Egypt becomes a positive symbol here of ancestral unity among African people and a reminder of the loss of their homeland. (5) Such phrases are contemporary and serve to link the past to the present day, thus appealing to a modern audience. (6) Answers will vary. A common interpretation is "female pride and empowerment." The speaker as depicted in first person and the repetition of her attributes and otherworldly talents and accomplishments focuses on her and her alone. The speaker's self-importance is an exaggeration in which she is representative of the entire female gender within the Black race. (7) Answers will vary. Students might connect the aspect of empowerment, tradition, and endurance of black females throughout history, coming to light in the present day with focus on gender and racial equality.

Activity #12 – Write Your Own Rap Song - Prewrite (All Grades). Responses will vary.

Activity #13 – Write Your Own Rap Song – Final Draft (All Grade Levels). Responses will vary.

Activity #14 – "Ode On a Grecian Urn" - First Read (All Levels): Student is to complete the worksheet "First Read Note Chart" adding notes, line number(s), rhyme scheme labels, and/or reactions to the text. Can write directly in the workbook, or print out additional charts from the templates located at the back of the workbook. A minimum of seven entries is suggested.

Rhyme Scheme: Divided into two parts with the final three lines of each stanza varying from the pattern. First seven lines – ABABCDE is used with consistency while the CDE section is not. Each verse is split into rhymes of four lines and six lines, respectively, which helps to create a division of two parts to each verse whereby the first four lines (ABAB) set up the verse's subject, and the final six lines allow the speaker to ponder what is meant.

Activity #15 – "Ode On a Grecian Urn" - Second Read (All Levels): Student is to complete the worksheet "Second Read Note Chart" adding key points, questions, identification of literary devices, and/or new reactions to the text. Can write directly in the workbook, or print out additional charts from the templates located at the back of the workbook. A minimum of seven entries is suggested.

Activity #16 – Writing Exercise -- Literary Analysis Paragraph (Grades 9-10): Responses will vary. Students should identify and discuss the central idea of the poem as being "the endurance of art over time". As the speaker contemplates the lives of the painted figures on the urn, he wonders about their lives and is both envious of their freedom from worry and toil, and at the same time, uneasy at seeing them as prisoners of their fate in the clay. Several depictions are shown, as the poem progresses that relay stories about the figures' lives that the speaker imagines, but in the end, do not matter. Humans are not everlasting – art, rather, is. **[See rubric for guidelines regarding writing form, style, and structure for paragraph].**

Activity #17 – Writing Exercise -- Literary Analysis Paragraph (Grades 11-12): Responses will vary. Students should attempt to explain the speaker's grappling with the paradox of the figures etched in the urn, seemingly frozen in time, unlike humans who are burdened with real lives. The artist gives the viewer of the art a lasting gift that will not perish. The "everlastingness" of art is the beauty of it. Art endures. The last two lines may appear like a riddle, which when pondered, are mysterious and as limiting as an inert piece of art. Because of this, it is understandable that the poet leaves the final interpretation up to the reader. **[See rubric for guidelines regarding writing form, style, and structure for paragraph].**

Activity #18 – "Social Media Post – Grecian Urn for Sale" – Creative Activity: Drawings will vary. Ad copy for Step #2 should resemble a compelling ad with details and buzzwords that accurately describe the Urn as drawn and would grab a customer's attention.

Activity #19 – "O Captain! O Captain!" - First Read (All Levels): Student is to complete the worksheet "First Read Note Chart" adding notes, line number(s), rhyme scheme labels, and/or reactions to the text. Can write directly in the workbook, or print out additional charts from the templates located at the back of the workbook. A minimum of seven entries is suggested.

Activity #20 – "O Captain! O Captain!" - Second Read (All Levels): Student is to complete the worksheet "Second Read Note Chart" adding key points, questions, identification of literary devices, and/or new reactions to the text. Can write directly in the workbook, or print out additional charts from the templates located at the back of the workbook. A minimum of seven entries is suggested.

Activity #21 – "O Captain! My Captain!" – Poem Translation (Grades 9-10): Answers will vary. Here is a sample summary:

Oh Captain, my Captain! Our hard journey has ended. The ship has survived every storm, and we've won the prize we've been fighting for. We are approaching the port and I can hear the bells clanging and the joyful celebration of the crowed. All eyes are on the adventurous ship that is both bold and brave. But oh, no! My heart is struck. Look at the drops of blood on the deck where my captain is lying cold and dead.

Oh Captain, my Captain! Get up! Can't you hear the bells and jubilation? Get up. They are waving the flag for you—the bugle is sounding in your honor. The people have brought bouquets and wreaths wrapped with ribbons for you—the shores are crowded with people who wish to honor you. They are calling for you, and all the people's eager faces are turning towards you. Here Captain! My dear father! Let me put my arm beneath your head. This is like a dream that you are lying here cold and dead.

My Captain is unable to answer me, as he is pale and still. His lips have no color and he cannot move. My father cannot feel my arm beneath his head, he is lifeless. The ship has anchored safely. It has accomplished its task. Its voyage had come to an end. This creates a joyful noise as the ship has weathered the journey and come home with the prize of victory. Let the crowds rejoice and the bells ring! But, too, sadness also has come as I walk in dreadful sorrow across the deck to where my Captain is lying cold and dead.

Activity #22 – Comprehension Questions (Grades 11-12): (1) b, (2) Abraham Lincoln, (3) d, (4) a, (5) b, (6) Examples: "My Captain does not answer, his lips are pale and still," and "he has no pulse nor will," and/or "my Captain lies, / Fallen cold and dead." (7) Answers will vary. The speaker is hoping to revive the captain and tries to help him to get up. (8) d.

Activity #23 – Writing Exercise -- Literary Analysis Paragraph (All Grades): Responses will vary. Students should identify and discuss the symbols in the poem as and how they contribute to the theme. The captain represents Abraham Lincoln as the leader of the Union, the ship and journey represent the struggle that was the Civil War, and the victory won. However, the joy and exultation are marred by the death of the nation's leader left lifeless on the deck. Students should include at least two passages from the poem with correct citation along with their analysis. **[See rubric for guidelines regarding writing form, style, and structure for paragraph].**

Activity #24 – Write An Elegy - (All Grades). Responses will vary. Literary devices should be used correctly and add to the impact of the poem.

Activity #25– "Annabel Lee" - First Read (All Levels): Student is to complete the worksheet "First Read Note Chart" adding notes, line number(s), rhyme scheme labels, and/or reactions to the text. Can write directly in the workbook, or print out additional charts from the templates located at the back of the workbook. A minimum of seven entries is suggested.

Activity #26 – "Annabel Lee" - Second Read (All Levels): Student is to complete the worksheet "Second Read Note Chart" adding key points, questions, identification of literary devices, and/or new reactions to the text. Can write directly in the workbook, or print out additional charts from the templates located at the back of the workbook. A minimum of seven entries is suggested.

Activity #27 – Vocabulary – (All Grades): (1) maiden (n) a girl or young woman, especially an unmarried one. (2) winged seraphs (n) an angelic being belonging to the highest order of celestial hierarchy; representative of light and purity. In the poem, the speaker believes that the angels are jealous of his and Annabel Lee's love and have caused her death (3) coveted (vb) to yearn to possess someone or something. (4) highborn (adj) pertaining to noble birth + kinsmen (n) a blood relation. In the poem, this is referring to Annabel Lee's relatives who might be looking down on the speaker for being of lesser status. (5) bore (vb) to make a hole in something as a drill through rock. (6) sepulcher (n) a small room or monument, cut in rock or stone, in which a deceased person is laid or buried. (7) envying (vb) to feel resentful or longing for someone else's possessions, qualities, or luck. (8) dissever (vb) to separate or divide; to break into parts. (9) beams (vb) to transmit or shine light brightly. (10) night-tide (n) a tide of the sea occurring at night.

Activity #28 – After Reading Questions (Grades 9-10): (1) They have known each other since childhood as stated, "I was a child and she was a child" (Line 7). The speaker says that the "winged seraphs of Heaven / Coveted her and me" (Lines 11-12). Further, that the angels, "Went envying her and me" (Line 22). Ultimately, the angels caused the cold wind to come and kill his beloved as, "the wind came out of the cloud by night, / Chilling and killing my Annabel Lee" (Lines 25-26). (3) The speaker says that "neither the angels in Heaven above / Nor the demons down under the sea" could separate the two loves' souls in life or death. (4) Nature is seen as both a force of death as Annabel Lee is "chilled" and "killed" by a cold wind that comes out of a "cloud by night; as well as a source of serenity and peace as when he describes, the "moon beams" which bring him dreams of his beloved and "stars never rise" without bringing him the feeling of her "bright eyes" and "all the night-tide" that brings with it the chance for him to "lie down beside" Annabel Lee. (5) In his mind, obsessed with thoughts of his deceased beloved, the speaker believes that he is able to recline with her at night "In her sepulcher" or tomb, by the sea. This suggests that he has not come to grips with the loss of his beloved.

Activity #28 – After Reading Questions (Grades 11-12): (1) Annabel Lee is described as a "young maiden" living in a "kingdom by the sea", which gives her the impression of being a type of fantasy figure in the speaker's mind (Lines 1-3. (2) The fact that the speaker recounts her childhood innocence gives off the sense that she was fragile and precious above all women—and angels, who envied her. In fact, she was so delicate that merely a chilly night-wind was enough to cause her to become ill and die. The speaker immortalizes her when he speaks of the dreams he continues to have of her noting her "bright eyes" and her ethereal beauty (Line 36). (3) The opening of the poem sets the tone of a sort of "fairy tale" as stated, "It was many and many a year ago, / In kingdom by the sea, / that a maiden there lived whom you may know / By the name of Annabel Lee" (Lines 1-4). Similar to fairy-tales, she has an adversary (the angels who covet her beauty and the two lovers' fortune). The story, however, does not have a happily ever after ending. The mythical coastal setting is dark and cold; it only offers moonlight and starlight in a sort of suspended reality. This mirrors the speaker's inability to escape from the darkness in his own mind that holds his thoughts prisoner in this cold, unforgiving place.

Activity #29 – Podcast Interview Questions (All Grade Levels). Responses will vary. Students should research the author and come up with 5-10 questions to "ask" him in a hypothetical podcast interview. Questions can be about his personal life, his works, and/or his take on modern-day poets and/or life in the current century.

Activity #30 – "My Last Duchess" - First Read (All Levels): Student is to complete the worksheet "First Read Note Chart" adding notes, line number(s), rhyme scheme labels, and/or reactions to the text. Can write directly in the workbook, or print out additional charts from the templates located at the back of the workbook. A minimum of seven entries is suggested.

Activity #31 – "My Last Duchess" - Second Read (All Levels): Student is to complete the worksheet "Second Read Note Chart" adding key points, questions, identification of literary devices, and/or new reactions to the text. Can write directly in the workbook, or print out additional charts from the templates located at the back of the workbook. A minimum of seven entries is suggested.

Activity #32 – "My Last Duchess" – Line Analysis (Grades 9-10): (1) Other strangers have also looked at the Duchess's painted portrait which only the Duke alone controls the revealing of it from behind the curtain. (2) The Duke is saying here that the blush on his Duchess's cheek, which others have commented on evident in the painting, and the delight that she felt that produced it, was not solely caused by him. (3) The fact that the Duchess expressed gratitude or acknowledged other men enraged the Duke; he could not understand how she did not prize his ancient name, or the privilege of being his wife, above the attentions of others or common delights (4) The Duke complains that his wife offered the same smile to him as to anyone who crossed her path. (5) The Duke arranged to have her killed and now personifies her being in the portrait that he boasts looks lifelike and hangs like a trophy on his wall. (6) The Duke instructs the Envoy to stand and move with him downstairs to meet the Count and his prospective future in-laws. He indicates that the dowry for his new bride will be sufficient. (7) The Duke is indicating that the Count's daughter is of interest to him as a wife. The Duke refers here to his potential future bride as "my object", which clearly shows his disregard for women and their individualism. (8) Here, the Duke is drawing attention to a statue of the god of sea exerting his power over a sea creature. Once again, he is exhibiting his wealth and "appreciation" for art in an effort to intimidate and manipulate.

The implication here is that he is relaying in a strong way to the Envoy a warning that his future intended and her family should know of his expectations, or suffer the consequences.

Activity #33 – "My Last Duchess" – Critical Thinking Questions (Grades 9-10): (1) The Duke is speaking to the emissary of the Count whose daughter is expected to be the Duke's next wife. The Envoy will be accompanying the Duke to meet with his potential new in-laws and others at a gathering downstairs. (2) The Duke despised that fact that it was not only himself that brought a blush of elation to her cheeks. She was easily moved by compliments and "too soon made glad" (Line 22) by the attentions of others, particularly, men. He felt that she was "too easily impressed" by simple happenings and things such as a brooch from him that she wore, a sunset, cherries on a bough, or the "white mule / She rode around the terrace" (Lines 23-29). He says that it was all the same to her. She liked everything and everyone in a way that produced the same blush on her cheek. He resented that she "thanked men—good!" (Line 31). She gave the same kindness to all, equally. (3) The Duke is a controlling, narcissistic, manipulator who views women as objects to be owned (like works of art). The Duke claims that his former Duchess did not respect his "gift of a nine-hundred-years-old name" (Line 33), rather, she regarded it with "anybody's gift" (Line 34). The manner in which the Duke commands the conversation with the Envoy, instructing him to sit and view the portrait that he alone controls the viewing of, is an example of how he is manipulating in nature. The Duke's speech, mannerisms, and modes of intimidation deliver a strong message that he did not allow his Duchess to express "approving speech, / Or blush, at least" (Lines 30-31) for anyone or anything other than himself. His cold tyranny is plain to see as when he casually says, "I gave commands; / Then all smiles stopped together" (Lines 45-46). His entire monologue serves as a warning to his new bride-to-be and her family; as he fully intends to make her his next and newest "possession." (4) The Duke has no regard for women as free-thinking individuals. He regards them as objects, like his works of art, which exist solely for his pleasure. The Duke resented the fact that the Duchess could be made happy by life's simple pleasures, and saw this as a threat to his control over her. When he says, "Who'd stoop to blame / This sort of trifling?" (Lines 34-35), he is asking rhetorically whether anyone would lower themselves to bring up the subject with someone in this situation to discuss it. He vows that such an exchange would be beneath him, "E'en then would be some stooping; and I choose / Never to stoop" (Lines 42-43). He could not even be bothered to let her know why she was to be punished with the worst of abuses. The reader is left to assume that his bride-to-be is of no deep consequence to him except in light of how she will serve at his will to be beautiful and compliant; like a fine piece of art.

Activity #34 – "My Last Duchess" – Poem Summary (Grades 11-12):

Answers will vary. The speaker of the poem, the Duke of Ferrara, is directing his guest's attention to a portrait of his former Duchess, "Looking as if she were alive" (Line 2). He refers to the piece as "a wonder" and boasts about how hard Fra Pandolf, the artist, worked on it. The Duke asks the Envoy to sit on a bench he has in place before the portrait so that he can look at the painting as the Duke drones on. The Duke draws back the curtain revealing the portrait and then quickly says that many strangers (more than one) have inquired as to how the artist was to capture the "depth and passion of [her] earnest glance" (Line 8). This is answered by the Duke with timing and precision as he says that it was not only he, her husband, that brought about the light to her eyes, or "that spot / Of joy into the Duchess' cheek" (Lines 14-15). He then surmises that perhaps it was the artist, Fra Pandolf, who might have complimented her in a way that produced her some bit of happiness that could be seen reflected as a "Half-flush" along her throat. The Duke points out that the former Duchess was all "too soon made glad" (Line 22) by the compliments of strangers and/or the simple things in life such as sunsets, cherry blossoms, and/or the white mule that she rode around the terrace. He found her to be too easily won over and much of everything in life made her equally happy. The Duke admonished her for "thanking men" for their kindnesses over her regard for his ancient name and status. He hesitates a bit to convey details (as if this is indeed the first time he is relaying the scene) and admonishes her for her lack of loyalty and devotion to him alone. He then asks rhetorically whether anyone would lower themselves to bring up the subject with someone in this situation to discuss it. He vows that such an exchange would be beneath him, "E'en then would be some stooping; and I choose / Never to stoop" (Lines 42-43). The Duke does express that although the Duchess did smile at him in passing, so too, she smiled at everyone else she encountered. It was when the smiles increased, he says, that he gave orders, "[And] then all smiles stopped together" (Line 46). It is presumed that he had her killed for this infraction. Now, there she "stands / As if alive" (Lines 46-47), a portrait of a woman who now only smiles at his command. The Duke then instructs the Envoy to rise from the bench in order to go downstairs to meet the other guests. The Duke reiterates to the Envoy that the Count's dowry for his daughter, the Duke's prospective bride-to-be, "Is ample warrant" as the Count's generosity is widely noted and the Duke is most certain that his "price" will be met in the arrangement. The Duke contends that his new bride-to-be is the ultimate prize, not the dowry. In this way, the Duke is assuring himself that in securing the perfect Duchess, he has won the ultimate spoils. The tour is ended and the two advance downstairs, but not before the Duke points out a statue—a work of art that Claus of Innsbruck sculpted depicting the god, Neptune, "Taming a sea-horse" (Line 55), which the Duke thinks a "rarity" as it was cast in bronze just for him. The message being that he, too, will dominate and control his prospective bride and in-laws. **[See rubric for guidelines regarding writing form, style, and structure for paragraph].**

Activity #35 – "My Last Duchess" – Critical Thinking Questions (Grades 11-12): (1) The Duke begins and maintains the monologue, controlling all aspects of the encounter. His speech is forward and commanding. There are no breaks or stanzas. The Duke loves to hear his own voice. There is no room for anyone else to talk. He quickly asks the Envoy, "Will't please you sit and look at her?" (Line 5). The Envoy has little choice and would not be able to get a word in edgewise if he wanted to. The Duke controls the curtain that reveals the portrait and every syllable uttered thereafter. He assumes that his guest is curious about the Duchess' "depth and passion" in her eyes and how such a glance came to be. The Duke is manipulative and cunning, even to the point of acting as if he is stumbling over his words in relaying his disbelief as to how his Duchess could disrespect him so as when he says, "A heart—how shall I say?—too soon made glad" (Line 22). His seemingly fragmented speech is most likely a well-tuned song which he has rehearsed and practiced many times to state his case. In this encounter though, it is clear that the underlying message is one of caution as he puts the Envoy, his future in-laws, and bride-to-be on notice that such infractions will not be tolerated.

(2) The Duke is bragging about his status and elitism as evidenced in his display of works of art and his interest in the reflection it has on him as a person of status. He wants to be clear that the artist is named for the value his work gives to the painting. This is not in tribute to the artist, but rather, a reflection on the Duke as a master of taste and procurement. In the final lines, the Duke makes sure that his guest takes notice of the sea-god Neptune taming a sea creature, which was "thought a rarity" (Line 55) and that Claus of Innsbruck cast for him in bronze.

(3) The painting of the Duchess symbolizes the Duke's status and his ability to "contain" the Duchess for his own will and pleasure. He regards all women as objects to be owned. In this case, all women are ornamental objects and he plans to make his new bride another one of his "possessions." The Duke delights is controlling who sees the portrait and in keeping her "earnest glance" all to himself. The portrait is also a symbol of the objectification of women in its most literal sense.

(4) The Duke points out to the Envoy, the bronze statue of Neptune taming a sea horse, "thought a rarity" (Lines 55). He brags that Claus of Innsbruck cast it in bronze for him. This is an unveiled threat to his future in-laws and bride-to-be that if his expectations are not met, he will dominate the next Duchess in the same unforgiving way. He will not tolerate disloyalty. It is every bit the Duke's intention to intimidate and warn his guest of his of his unwavering expectations with the message that he will not be tested.

Activity #36 – Pick a Persona – Journal Writing (All Grades): Responses will vary. Students with choose ONE persona to work with in drafting a creative written response in a letter or journal format. All conventions of proper spelling, sentence structure, grammar and punctuation applies.

Activity #37 – Concrete Poems – Create Your Own Concrete Poem (All Grades): Responses will vary. The visual appearance should match the topic/theme of the poem. It does not have to rhyme.

Activity #38 – Haiku – Write Your Own Haiku Poems (All Grades): Responses will vary. Students should adhere to the traditional Japanese format of seventeen syllables in a 5, 7, and 5-syllable pattern.

Activity #39 – "Song of America" - First Read (All Levels): Student is to complete the worksheet "First Read Note Chart" adding notes, line number(s), repeated patterns, and/or reactions to the text. Can write directly in the workbook, or print out additional charts from the templates located at the back of the workbook. A minimum of seven entries is suggested.

Activity #40 – "Song of America" - Second Read (All Levels): Student is to complete the worksheet "Second Read Note Chart" adding key points, questions, identification of literary devices, and/or new reactions to the text. Can write directly in the workbook, or print out additional charts from the templates located at the back of the workbook. A minimum of seven entries is suggested.

Activity #41 – Short Answer Questions (Grades 9-10): (1) The speaker is addressing the people not only in New York, but the nation. This is an anthem of hope for all of America in a time of crisis. (2) During the pandemic of 2020, there were great depletions of goods in the supermarkets; directives for lock-downs caused the streets and hallways of schools and offices to be empty. (3) Even though Americans were sheltered in place and cut off from each other, the speaker is calling for people's hearts to remain open and to not grow cold and hard as a result of fear and panic. The most heroic thing that people could do at that point was to wait. (4) The speaker is asking the people of America to hold on to hope and to "rise" up in spirit together; to see the common unity this calamity has brought, allowing one nation to band together like never before. (5) In the final stanza, the speaker evokes God almighty as one who measures out "life's joyful songs." This, too, is a song or experience that tests one and all. The same God at whose hand has brought His people through tough times can bring all rescue and vigilance once again. America is a shinning nation that embraces the light.

Activity #42 – After Reading Questions (Grades 11-12): (1) It is clear that the speaker is distressed and even at a loss for words in trying to relay his or her feelings. As stated, "How can I put into words what / I am seeing, feeling, fearing?" Clearly, the speaker is in the situation as well and is at first, trying to sort out all of the changes that the pandemic is imposing on the nation. The speaker goes on to admit that it is like a "dream" and a "gruesome test" challenging every American to their limits. In stanza seven, the mood shifts to that of hope as, "In this harrowing hour / Hold fast, rise up, be strong" (Lines 31-32), suggesting that in what seems to be America in a fragile state, is only a precursor to her "hidden power" (Line 33). (2) The free writing form helps to create a sense of disorder and or "chaos" of a city struggling to "rise from the scourge," which is New York, the gateway to the world. This is not the normal "hum" of the city as it is know for, rather a disorder which delivers, "Daily blows of shock and grief" in the rising COVID deaths. It is a battlefield of a different kind for America to contemplate. The author puts in deliberate runs of rhyme scheme that serve to provide some structure in the chaos and to produce a type of rhythm or drum beat in the background of the bedlam. Verses form a type of further structure to the words and tower like Lady Liberty herself held firm at the base (the poem's final stanza) with the assurance of heavenly intervention. The repetitive chant, "Oh brother, Oh, sister—" humanizes the message and places the speaker in the situation along with fellow Americans. (3) The COVID pandemic has emptied the "shelves, streets, and halls" and closed the doors to the outside world, threatening to "shutter" Americans' hearts to the joys and freedoms all have known. Rising numbers of deaths have threatened to shatter spirits and it seems as if grief is the only common thread holding people together. The speaker urges Americans to rise above by either "fate or grace" to endure and to find in oneself—strength, acknowledging that both the "very worst" and the "very best" reside in us all (Line 23). This is a battle cry to carry on through the "sorrow, fear, and pain" just as the essential workers (masked angels) persevere when the task seems impossible. The final two stanzas are a call to rise up and to recognize the "hidden power" all Americans have claim to from "He who counts our days and hours" (Line 34). All Americans should remain steadfast in the face of adversity because this is a battle of the ages that will not be fought alone.

Activity #43 – Write Your Own Free Verse Poem - Prewrite (All Grades). Responses will vary.

Activity #44 – Write Your Own Free Verse Poem – Final Draft (All Grades). Responses will vary.

Activity #45 – Poetry Exam (Grades 9-10): (1) b, (2) a, (3) b, (4) a, (5) a, (6) b, (7) b & c, (8) d, (9) d, (10) Lyric, Narrative, Dramatic (11) T, (12) T, (13) F, (14) T, (15) T, (16) T (17) a, (18), b, (19) b, (20) d, (21) **Answers will vary. Here is a sample summary:**

I am feeling happy and joyful as I begin to embark on a journey on foot. I am feeling "healthy and free" from constraints and embrace the destiny that I control in terms of where I go. I do not seek fortune from anyone or anything; rather, I create my own good-fortune. There is nothing that I am lacking. This new mindset I am taking will not allow for negativity or delays even though I know that this road will have its own challenges. I will not need for anything on this journey. The universe will provide all that I need, when I need it. No longer will others' complaints or quarrels affect me. I am strong and can carry any burden; confident as I set forth forward on the road to my destination.

(22) A, (23) C, (24) C. (25) Concrete Poem, (26) Free Verse, (27) Dramatic monologue, (28) Haiku, (29) Narrative, (30) Hip Hop, (31) Ode.

Activity #46 – Poetry Exam (Grades 11-12): (1) b, (2) a, (3) b, (4) a, (5) a, (6) b, (7) b & c, (8) d, (9) d, (10) Lyric, Narrative, Dramatic (11) T, (12) T, (13) F, (14) T, (15) T, (16) T (17) a, (18), b, (19) b, (20) d, (21) b, (22) c, (23) **Answers will vary. Students should include lines from the text, properly cited within their response. Example:** The comparison of the sun setting in the sky to the "parting of old acquaintances / Who bow over their clasped hands" (Line 8) depicts a closing out or ending of something coming to completion. The day's end is inevitable, just as this parting of two friends who must journey onward. The gesture of bowing seems to affirm their acceptance with the fact that they are bidding farewell.

(24) Concrete poem, (25) Free Verse, (26) Dramatic monologue, (27) Haiku, (28) Narrative, (29) Hip Hop, (30) Ode, (31) Shakespearean sonnet (32) c, (33) d, (34) b, (35)

Answers will vary. Some responses might include: The wheelbarrow is a representation of agricultural life and/or farm workers, indicating a respect and appreciation for the labor of those who provide food for the nation; a useful tool or object that might cause the reader to form an appreciation for simplicity and a slower pace in life. By pausing to look at a simple item, this might inspire the reader to contemplate how he or she "sees" or "fails to see" different things in their life.

(36) **Answers will vary. Some responses might include:** The sparse text and lack of punctuation gives the poem a casual feel, free from restrictions; this enables the reader to linger over the words that are spread out and stand alone at times for emphasis and fluidity. The blank spaces around the words offer the reader an opportunity to "think" and affords time to contemplate and to feel appreciation for the object. The lack of end punctuation further suggests that the reader should not stop at this one object, but should seek opportunities to ponder the wonders in other seemingly simple items in life.

(37) Answers will vary. Students should choose one theme to discuss in a well-formed paragraph that includes in-text citations with their analysis. **[See rubric for guidelines regarding writing form, style, and structure for paragraph].**

(38) b, (39) c, (40) a, (41) a, (42) **Answers will vary. A sample response might include:**

America is my home. She feeds me bitterness and attacks me as with a wild animal's strength, making it difficult for me to breathe. Although America is a place that tests me to the core, I draw from her vast, powerful torments and rise up against the hate and bigotry that comes in punishing waves. At the same time her strength flows through my bones. However, unlike a dissident soldier who rises up against a brutal king, I rather, find shelter in her walls, and speak no tyranny against these great injustices. The dark days ahead are certain; the hand of unrelenting time that marches on will test the limits of her "granite wonders," and will see her borders, like precious jewels, fade into oblivion.

(43) **Answers will vary. A sample response might include:**

McKay's "love-hate" relationship with America is evident in this very complex paradox of emotions that brings him to both fear and revere her for her powers. She can both destroy him and enliven him at the same time. At best, he is able to see with clear eyes that such a nation might not withstand the oppression and brutality of her dual-nature. As with a broken heart, the speaker is made stronger by the abuse and left fiercer as a result of having survived the fight. He loves "this cultured hell that tests my youth" (Line 4); in spite of the fact that he is defenseless to her taking something away from him that he can never get back. His eerie prediction; however, of his country falling beneath the "touch of Time's unerring hand," suggests that in the end, he is able to endure in a way that she will not. Thus, helping him to balance out the difficult reality of her injustices.

(44) **Answers will vary. A sample response might include:**

In the poem, "America," the speaker professes to love his new country despite the fact that she "feeds [him] bread of bitterness" and "sinks [her] tiger's tooth" into his neck (McKay, lines 1-2). Within her borders, America "tests" his youth and yet fortifies him to withstand her assaults of prejudice and hate. In this way, he both loves and despises her in a paradox of emotions. His reverence for America is solely due to the strength she has given him to withstand her blows and see her for what she is—a country comprised of fear, hate, and privilege. In "Song of America," the speaker is not judgmental about America or her people. Rather, it is the pandemic, an outside force, that is the "gruesome test" that causes all to "hold fast, rise up, [and] be strong" (Collins, lins 32). In this way, it is a merciless intrusion that threatens a modern-day America in the face of adversity' The "daily blows of shock and grief" are felt by all Americans and thus unites them (Collins, line 14). There is compassion and reverence for Lady Liberty who "seems to shed a thousand tears" but who is depicted as "rising from the scourge" rather succumbing to it (Collins, lines 8-9). Namely, it is the people of all walks of life and ideologies who are given the promise of hope and "rescue" in "this harrowing hour," united (Collins, lines 31-33). Both speakers acknowledge America as a great wonder with "priceless treasures" to behold, but it is clear that the first poem, "America" dooms her to fall under the weight of her transgressions, while "Song of America" finds her made stronger as a result of hardship.

Rubric for Literary Paragraph

CATEGORY	Distinguished 4	Proficient 3	Approaching 2	Needs Improvement 1
Introduction	The title and author are correctly introduced and the topic is clearly stated in the paragraph.	The title and author are included. The topic is clearly stated.	The title and/or author are not included. The topic is not stated clearly.	The title and/ or author are not included. The topic/meaning is not stated.
Interpretation	The student is able to identify and explain the literary element(s) in the poem.	The literary element(s) is/ are clearly explained.	Literary element(s) are stated but do not connect to the analysis.	The literary element(s) are not identified or explained in relation to the poem.
Analysis	Insightful, supported analysis in conjunction with passages from the text correctly cited.	The analysis is insightful and supported by passages from the text.	The analysis is confusing and does not connect with the passage from the text.	The analysis is weak and/or too brief; it does not address the prompt and/or connect to the text.
Evidence	There are at least two pieces of evidence from the text, in quotation marks, which support the student's commentary.	There is one piece of evidence from the text. The evidence is not enclosed in quotation marks.	There is one piece of evidence from the text, but it is not enclosed in quotation marks.	There is no evidence provided in the paragraph.
Sentence structure, verb tense, voice	Uses logic and flow of ideas; present tense analysis.	Use of logic and flow of ideas effectively; analysis is not in present tense.	Some errors in logic and /or flow of ideas; analysis is not in present tense.	Errors in logic and/or no flow of ideas; analysis not in present tense.
Writing Skills & Mechanics	Spelling, capitalization, and grammar rules present in analysis.	The writing has 2-3 grammar errors. Slang or contractions present.	The writing has 4-5 grammar errors. Slang or contractions present.	The writing has over 5 mistakes in grammar, punctuation, and/ or spelling. Slang or contractions present.

Total Points: _____ / 24

Resource: Literary Terms

Alliteration: The repetition of identical consonant sounds, most often the sounds beginning words in close proximity. Example: **p**ensive **p**oets.

Allusion: Unacknowledged references and/or quotations that authors assume their readers will recognize.

Anaphora: Repetition of the same word or phrase at the beginning of a line throughout a work or the section of a work. Example: "O Captain! My Captain!"

Apostrophe: Speaker in a poem addresses a person not present or an animal, inanimate object or concept as though it is a person. Example: Wordsworth—"Milton! Thou shouldst be living at this hour / English has need of thee."

Assonance: The repetition of identical vowel sounds in different words in close proximity. Example: d**ee**p gr**ee**n s**ea**.

Ballad: A narrative poem composed of quatrains (iambic tetrameter alternating with iambic trimester) rhyming x-a-x-a.

Blank Verse: Unrhymed iambic pentameter. Example: Shakespeare's plays.

Consonance: The counterpart of assonance; the partial or total identity of consonants in words whose main vowels differ. Example: shadow meadow; pressed, passed; sipped supped.

Couplet: Two successive rhyming lines. Couplets end the pattern of a Shakespearean sonnet.

Diction: Diction is usually used to describe the level of formality that a speaker uses.

Dramatic monologue: A type of poem, derived from the theater, in which a speaker addresses an internal listener or the reader. In some dramatic monologues, especially those by Robert Browning, the speaker may reveal his personality in unexpected and unflattering ways.

End-stopped line: A line ending in a full pause, usually indicated with a period or semicolon.

Enjambment: A line having no end punctuation but running over to the next line.

Foot: A measured combination of heavy and light stresses. The numbers of feet are monometer (1) foot), dimeter (2 feet), trimester (3 feet), tetrameter (4 feet), pentameter (5 feet), hexameter (6 feet), heptameter or septenary (7 feet).

Form: The physical structure of a poem; the length of lines, their rhythms, their system of rhymes and repetition.

Hyperbole: Exaggeration for effect.

Iambic pentameter: An unstressed stressed foot. The most natural and common kind of meter in English; it elevates speech to poetry.

Image: Images are references that trigger the mind to fuse together memories of sight (visual), sounds (auditory), tastes (gustatory), smells (olfactory), and sensations of touch (tactile). Imagery refers to images throughout a work or throughout the works of a writer or group of writers.

Internal rhyme: An exact rhyme (rather than rhyming vowel sounds, as with assonance) within a line of poetry: "Once upon a midnight **dreary**, while I pondered, weak and **weary**."

Metaphor: A comparison between two unlike things, this describes one thing as if it were something else. Does not use "like" or "as" for the comparison.

Meter: The number of feet within a line of traditional verse. Example: iambic pentameter.

Onomatopoeia: A blending of consonant and vowel sounds designed to imitate or suggest activity being described. Example: buzz, slurp.

Paradox: A rhetorical figure embodying a seeming contradiction that is nonetheless true.

Parallelism: The repetition of grammatical elements in writing and speaking. In poetry can be used to create a childish sing-song tone, build tension or emphasize a point.

Personification: Attributing human characteristics to nonhuman things or abstractions.

Petrarchan sonnet: A sonnet (14 lines of rhyming iambic pentameter) that divides into an octave (8) and sestet (6). There is a "volta," or "turning" of the subject matter between the octave and sestet.

Poetic license: A poet's departure from the rules of grammar, syntax, and vocabulary in order to maintain a metrical or rhyme scheme; can also mean the manipulation of facts to suit the needs of a poem.

Refrain: Repeated word or series of words in response or counterpoint to the main verse, as in a ballad.

Repetition: The use of the same word or phrase multiple times, whereby creating a pattern through rhythm.

Rhyme: The repetition of identical concluding syllables in different words, most often at the ends of lines. Example: June—moon.

Run-on lines: A running on of a thought from one line to another without final punctuation.

Slant rhyme: A near rhyme in which the concluding consonant sounds are identical but not the vowels. Example: sun/noon, should/food, slim/ham.

Sestet: A six-line stanza or unit of poetry.

Shakespearean sonnet: A fourteen-line poem written in iambic pentameter, composed of three quatrains and a couplet rhyming abab cdcd efef gg.

Simile: A direct comparison between two dissimilar things; uses "like" or "as" to state the terms of the comparison.

Sonnet: A closed form consisting of fourteen lines of rhyming iambic pentameter.

Stanza: A group of poetic lines corresponding to paragraphs in prose; the meters and rhymes are usually repeating or systematic.

Symbol: A person, object, place, event, or action that suggests more than its literal meaning.

Syntax: Word order and sentence structure.

Tone: The poet's attitude toward the poem's speaker, reader, and subject matter, as interpreted by the reader.

Volta: The "turning" point of a Petrarchan sonnet, usually occurring between the octave and the sestet.

Shake Shock Press books are available at special discounts when purchased in bulk for fund-raising or educational use. For details visit the Shake Shock Press website at www.jamiecollinsteacher.com.

Also by Shake Shock Press:

Quick Lit Student Workbook –
Study of Language Arts: The Short Story

Quick Lit –
A Collection of Short Stories

For more information, or to book Jamie Collins for media events or interviews, email at contact@jamiecollinsauthor.com.

www.ingramcontent.com/pod-product-compliance
Lightning Source LLC
Chambersburg PA
CBHW051211290426
44109CB00021B/2421